Before ordination, James Jones was a teacher, then an audio-visual producer. After 12 years in parish ministry in Bristol and Croydon he became Bishop of Hull in 1994 and then Bishop of Liverpool in 1998.

He is heavily involved in urban regeneration, chairing the government's New Deal for Communities in Liverpool. The Bishop also chairs the North West Constitutional Convention and the board of a new faith-based City Academy. One of his major interests is in the role of the churches and the voluntary sector in community renewal.

He sees the environment as central to the mission of God.

His other books, including *Why Do People Suffer?* (Lion) and *The Moral Leader* (IVP) reflect his concern to relate Christianity to contemporary culture.

Bishop James broadcasts regularly and chairs Wycliffe Hall in Oxford. He is married to Sarah and they have three daughters – Harriet, Jemima and Tabitha.

To
the people in the parishes
of the
Diocese of Liverpool

Jesus and the Earth

JAMES JONES

First published in Great Britain in 2003 by
Society for Promoting Christian Knowledge
Holy Trinity Church
Marylebone Road
London NW1 4DU

British Library Cataloguing-in-Publication Data
A catalogue record for this book is available from the British
Library

ISBN 0-281-05623-4

10 9 8 7 6 5 4 3 2 1

Designed and typeset by Kenneth Burnley, Wirral, Cheshire
Printed in Great Britain by Bookmarque Ltd, Croydon, Surrey

Contents

Preface

I am grateful to the Trustees of the Galt Lectures and especially to the Revd Jeffrey Fishwick for the generous invitation to give the annual Galt Lectures in March 2003 in Charlottesville, Virginia, USA. The response to these lectures has been a major encouragement to me to make them available in print.

My wife Sarah bears the brunt of all my travelling, both managing the needs of the family and supervising life at Bishop's Lodge. She more than any has been both surprised and delighted at my ecological conversion. She looks forward to seeing me move from theory to practice – especially in the garden of our cottage!

I am indebted to Margaret Funnell, my Personal Assistant, and to Wendy Trussell, our Assistant Secretary, for their patient and imaginative interpretation of all my scribblings.

These chapters, brief and simple though they are, arose initially out of various conferences sponsored by Christian Ecology Link and the John Ray Institute. I am still a novice in all these things and am honoured to have sat at the feet of some magisterial minds and practitioners such as Sir John Houghton, Professor Sam Berry, Sir Martin Holdgate and Sir Jonathon

Porritt. In gratitude I have included one of each of their books in the further reading list on p. 102 in the hope that you might benefit as much as I have.

Every now and again you read a book which you can describe in no other way than 'life changing'! *Soil and Soul* by Alastair McIntosh is such. It was one of the first that I read as I entered the field hedged in by both ecology and theology. It provided a map for my journey. Conversations with the author by e-mail and in person have made a great impact on me.

I thank too the Diocese of Liverpool; also my colleagues in the Core Group, especially David Jennings, the Bishop of Warrington, who really do believe and support me in my belief that the Diocesan Bishop should take time to think creatively. The clergy and the people of this Diocese live their lives with passion and compassion, with faith and faithfulness, with humour and humanity. It is both humbling and inspiring to be their Bishop.

No record of gratitude would be complete without mentioning Phil Leigh, my Lay Assistant and Environmental Adviser. With his degree in ecology and his own love of nature he has accompanied me on many journeys. Countless conversations with him have enabled me to fertilize my reading of the Bible with the organic compost of his ecological understanding! To shift from organic to mechanical imagery: the dialogue between us has been the beginning of a bolting together of theology and ecology, which for too long have been allowed to exist independently of each other. Phil, with Tom, is also the gardener at Bishop's Lodge. Of all his responsibilities he holds this to be his highest calling.

Preface

I hope this small book might fall into the hands of some aspiring theologians who, with their supervisors, will see that there is some merit in doing a Ph.D. on the unique collection of the Son of Man and the earth sayings in the Gospels. I know of nothing in this area so far. Ph.Ds have been done on less substantial foundations.

I am very conscious of the inadequacy of the work that follows and know that it merits more examination than I can give. Part of me would love to take three years to study at depth. Yet another part of me knows that what I am and what I here contribute is shaped uniquely by the engagement I have in urban mission as Bishop of Liverpool. It is the people here, not least in Kensington where I have chaired the New Deal for Communities, that have taught me, more than they realize, about the connection between the gospel and the earth, the Word and the world.

THE RT REVD JAMES JONES
Trinity 2003

Chapter 1

The Son of Man Has Authority On Earth

When I was a student reading theology there was a popular joke:

> Jesus said to Peter, 'Who do people say that I am?'
> Peter said to Jesus, 'You are the eschatological manifestation of the ground of our being'.
> Jesus said to Peter, 'You what?'

It pokes fun at how theological language and concepts can be so remote from ordinary lives. Who on earth knows the meaning of eschatology? Well, it may not be widely understood, yet it could become the dominant theological concept that will push off the shelves all other '-ologies', from ecclesiology to pneumatology. Why? Because it is the study of the end, a look into the future. To put it into popular speak, 'What on earth will happen to the earth?' or, to give the question a theological slant, 'What in heaven's name will become of the earth?'

Top ten terrible things

The instability of the Middle East could have the same devastating consequences on the international body of nations as a burst appendix. Certainly since 11 September 2001 or '9/11' (is it significant that this tragic event has no name or title except a date?) ordinary people have become more aware of their insecurity and of the fragility of the world. International terrorism, weapons of mass destruction, global market collapse, financial crises, epidemics, disappearance of animal species, pollution of the seas and atmosphere, exploitation of natural resources to the point of extinction: all present the ingenuity of the human family with the challenge of survival. You don't have to be a pathological pessimist to begin to wonder where and how all this will end. The media have already begun to ask the question. In the UK, Bryan Appleyard in the *Sunday Times* explored in a major feature the 'Top Ten Terrible Things' that might happen to the world, and a major British TV drama series, *The Second Coming* by the atheist Russell T. Davies, wondered how the Son of God might come again to the earth.

Recently I saw a bumper-sticker on the back of a lorry: 'JESUS IS COMING – LOOK BUSY!' My daughters tell me there are fashionable t-shirts with the same message. Thoughts even within popular culture seem to be turning to the end of the world.

Just as we were getting over the threat of weapons of mass destruction after the end of the Iraq war, a deadly and invisible virus struck. SARS soon displaced Saddam as the threat to world order. Panic gripped Beijing, Hong Kong's airport was deserted, Toronto was made a no-go area by the World Health Organization, and the global economy took another body blow.

This was not just 'tabloid terror'. Serious minds are

beginning to ask radical questions about our ability to survive. Martin Rees, the Astronomer Royal and renowned astro-physicist, has written a new book called *Our Final Century: Will the Human Race survive the 21st Century?* His conclusion is that we have a 50–50 chance of survival. He says that although we should be able to feed the hungry, save the planet and redistribute power globally, 'We are . . . empowering more people with the potentiality to harm on an ever-growing scale.'

This is bleak stuff! But it's good for religion! I have often said that when it comes to getting people to turn to God, it's not a mission strategy that will do it, but a disaster! Don't think me cynical or irresponsible. It's just that the enemy of faith in God is human self-sufficiency. It's only when this illusion is shattered that we open up to who we are and why on earth we're on this planet. My guess is that as the threats to our existence multiply, so more and more will turn to hear what different religions, including the Church, have to say about the future.

Christian theologians have distinctive contributions to make. For example, John Polkinghorne's *The God of Hope and the End of the World* takes us gently yet resolutely to the edge to contemplate the future. I believe there will be a renewed popular interest in what different sacred scriptures have to say about our destiny, both personal and global. Within Christianity there will be – indeed it has already started – a revisiting of the Bible to learn what it says about the end of the world. In America, popular novels about the end of the world have topped the bestseller lists.

Nature is never spent?

But these are not new questions. The poet Gerard Manley Hopkins was facing them in his famous poem 'God's grandeur':

> The world is charged with the grandeur of God.
> It will flame out, like shining from shook foil;
> It gathers to a greatness, like the ooze of oil
> Crushed. Why do men then now not reck his rod?
> Generations have trod, have trod, have trod;
> And all is seared with trade; bleared, smeared with
>   toil;
> And wears man's smudge and shares man's smell:
>   the soil
> Is bare now, nor can foot feel, being shod.
>
> And for all this, nature is never spent;
> There lives the dearest freshness deep down things;
> And though the last lights off the black West went
> Oh, morning, at the brown brink eastward,
>   springs –
> Because the Holy Ghost over the bent
> World broods with warm breast and with ah!
>   bright wings.

I wonder whether after the Johannesburg Summit, Hopkins would have written so optimistically, 'Nature is never spent'? It is the big ecological question: Have we passed the point of no return? Does the earth possess the power to heal itself? Does there still live 'the dearest freshness deep down things'?

What would Jesus say?

The purpose of this book has a specific focus. It asks simply what was the attitude of Jesus to the earth. It is based on a conviction that to discern Christ's attitude to the earth would be formative in shaping the outlook of those who learn from him under his authority.

When it comes to ethics of the environment, or what could be called an earth-ethic, Christians often turn to the pages of the Old Testament. I was recently asked to write the preface to a booklet on sustainable development by a leading evangelical charity. All the biblical references in this pamphlet came from the Old Testament; there were none from the Gospels.

In a conversation with the Chief Rabbi about Jewish environmental ethics, when I quizzed him about Genesis he dismissed this (ever so graciously) as a typically Christian way of handling the Bible! He went to the pages of Deuteronomy and to the law that forbade the invading forces to destroy any fruit-bearing tree as they lay siege to the cities of the Promised Land. On the nicety of this legal point did the Jewish teachers construct an ethic about the environment.

For various reasons (both personal and theological – and, to be honest, it is sometimes difficult to disentangle the two!) when it came to my study leave I wanted to see what the Gospels revealed of Jesus' attitude to the earth. My own spirituality has, since I was a boy, been heartily focused on Jesus. I read, translate and study the Gospels nearly every day. As I became more intensely aware of the critical issues facing the earth, not least through my encounters with young people, I found myself urgently enquiring whether this concern found any sympathy in the teaching and example of Jesus.

In the millennium year 2000, I travelled the Diocese and in every Deanery visited the largest secondary school. I asked the head teacher if I could meet with 16–18-year-olds to listen to their dreams and dreads of the future and to say why I thought that Jesus Christ was still relevant today.

The door of every school opened and sometimes there were over 250 students. We produced three short videos to stimulate discussion on the future of the earth, relationships and the spiritual search. After the video clip of the environment I asked them on a scale of 0 to 10 to say how worried they were about the future of the planet. In every school 100 per cent of hands went up with students putting themselves between 5 and 10. I then asked them, again on a scale of 0 to 10, to what extent they felt we *ought* to do something about it. I drew attention to the moral word 'ought' and again found that 98 per cent of all hands went up.

I came away impressed by these young people's sense of morality and their commitment to the environment. Adults will, of course, at this stage point to the fact that the same young people might well go on to drop litter in the street. But in this they are no different from their seniors, who can also and equally adeptly say one thing and do another! The passionate concern of these thousands of young people sent me back to the Bible to see if their moral priorities found any echoes in scripture and, in particular, in the teachings of Jesus.

Precious little?

Up until my study leave, if you had asked me what Jesus had to say about the earth and whether the Gospels had anything to say in formulating an environmental ethic, I would have thought 'precious little'. However, all that has changed. I have read the Gospels again and again, and am still reading. I am determined to read out of the text and not into it. I find myself unearthing things in the Gospels which persuade me that Jesus not only was earthed but also saw his mission as none other than the earthing of heaven. 'Your will be done on earth as it is in heaven' was the logical *sequitur* of his prayer for the coming of the Kingdom. This book is a reflection on my search for evidence of the connectedness of Jesus to the earth and begins in the stormiest of waters and with the furious debates over what Jesus meant when he called himself 'The Son of Man'. It is the only title that he takes to himself. He affirms acclamations that he is the Son of God, Lord and God and cautiously acknowledges that he is the Christ, the Messiah. Yet when it comes to describing himself, he exclusively uses the phrase 'Son of Man'.

It was in the same conversation with the Chief Rabbi that he reminded me that in Hebrew the phrase 'Son of Man' is Ben Adam, Son of Adam, and Adam is the one hewn from the earth, *Adamah* in Hebrew. I returned to the Gospel text with a new eagerness. Searching for evidence of a connectedness between Jesus and the earth I took special notice of those episodes in which he called himself the 'Son of Man' and wondered whether I would find there any echoes of Adam or *Adamah*, the earth. Every time I came across a 'Son of Man' saying I wrote down the verse and marked it in red. Then a remarkable question intruded upon my thinking. It felt like an intrusion, for it seemed to come out of the blue, or at least at an angle to my linear thought processes at the time. 'Are there any occasions when Jesus calls himself the Son of Man and in the same breath or in the same context talks about the earth?' There are! As I read through the Gospels again I wrote down every reference to the earth and marked them in green.

(Those with CD-Rom will find this not such a laborious task! By the way, there are 863 references to the earth in the whole Bible and 165 in the New Testament. Those interested in numerical detail will surely be impressed that this compares with 494 references to heaven and 537 references to love. The number of references shows that the Bible is as interested in the earth as much as it is in heaven.)

I discovered to my surprise that there are at least seven occasions when the green and red marks appear together where we come across the earth mentioned in the same context as the Son of Man. I hesitate to use the word 'excitement' for it is heavily overworked in some circles, but I was genuinely excited by this discovery and read the Gospels, especially these seven passages, with all the eagerness of a new convert. Here they are (the italics are mine):

1 'The *Son of Man* has authority on *earth* to forgive sins' (Matthew 9.2–8).
2 'The *Son of Man* will be in the heart of the *earth*' (Matthew 12.38–42).
3 'The sign of the *Son of Man* will appear in heaven and then all the tribes on *earth* will mourn' (Matthew 24.27–30).

4 '[God] will quickly grant justice to them. And yet when the *Son of Man* comes will he find faith on *earth*?' (Luke 18.8).

5 'For it will come upon all who live on the face of the whole *earth*. Be alert at all times praying that you may have the strength . . . to stand before the *Son of Man*' (Luke 21.35–6).

6 'The hour has come for the *Son of Man* to be glorified. Very truly I tell you, unless a grain of wheat falls into the *earth* and dies, it remains just a single grain . . .' (John 12.23–4).

7 'When I am lifted up from the *earth* I will draw all to myself . . . How can you say the *Son of Man* must be lifted up?' (John 12.32–4).

(See also Matthew 16.13–19; Mark 14.35–41; Luke 12.39–51; John 3.11–15.)

Every theologian I have talked to has urged me to be cautious about the significance of this and about assuming that Jesus would have been conscious of the adam/*adamah* root to the designation 'Son of Man'. What is clear is that this is the only title, if it is that, which he takes to himself. Is it, as Geza Vermes argues, simply a circumlocution for the personal pronoun 'I' or does it, as Walter Wink in his recently published *The Human Being* argues, signify a title? And if it does and has its roots in Old Testament usage, is it Daniel or Ezekiel or Genesis or the Psalms that are being evoked? However debatable that question is, what is indisputable is that Paul clearly saw a defining relationship between Jesus and Adam (Romans 5 and 1 Corinthians 15). But was this ever in the mind of Jesus or even the writers of the Gospels?

And if so, is it to be found in his unique self-reference as Son of Man, a title that Paul never uses of him?

Of the passages in the Gospels where the Son of Man and the earth are explicitly mentioned together, let us look at three, one each from Luke, Matthew, and John.

Authority on earth

The Lucan passage occurs in all three synoptic Gospels. It is the story of the forgiving and healing of a person paralysed and incapable of walking. Having absolved him, Jesus says to him and his critics, 'The Son of Man has authority on earth to forgive sins' (Luke 5.24).

Each synoptic Gospel account includes the reference to the earth. Why 'on earth'? What is added to the meaning of his authority to forgive by stating explicitly that it was 'on earth'? Many avenues of enquiry are opened up by this question. By suggesting one in particular I am not suggesting the closing down of others. If (and I know the enormity of two-letter words however provisional they are in reality), if the title 'Son of Man' had any allusion to Adam, to *adamah* and the earth, one avenue of enquiry would lead us to the opening chapters of Genesis. The context of this saying of Jesus is the forgiving of the paralysed man, 'Son, your sins are forgiven.' Once in Genesis the mention of sin takes us directly to the disobedience of the first Adam, the sin and its consequences. But is there any mention of the earth in the story of Adam's falling into sin? There is, of course. The result of their sin is that the earth is cursed. Adam who was hewn from the earth and called to serve the earth (Genesis 2.7, 15) finds that his sin wreaks havoc on the earth: 'cursed is the ground because of you' (3.17).

The only way that the earth can be relieved of its curse is through the forgiveness, healing and restoration of Adam's successors. It is not only Christian, Muslim and Jewish theologians who would concur with this view. Countless environmentalists, pressure groups and lobbyists would testify to the truth that the wholeness of the earth and the future of the planet depend upon the repentance and restoration to wholeness of the human family. John McNeill's *Something New Under the Sun* shows how human folly and greed are responsible for the disease of the earth. Bjørn Lomborg, in his book *The Skeptical Environmentalist*, has sought to undermine these anxieties and received widespread publicity. However, his own scientific methods and conclusions have been dismissed as flawed by the Danish Committee on Scientific Dishonesty. You don't have to believe in God to believe the biblical adage 'You reap what you sow.' The earth bears the wounds of human sinfulness. 'The whole creation has been groaning,' says Paul, clinging to the 'hope that the creation itself will be set free from its bondage to decay' (Romans 8.21, 22).

The future wholeness of the earth and the whole of creation according to Paul is bound up with the destiny of the children of God. A redeemed humanity is central to that vision. Key to that redemption is God's forgiveness. In short, how can the earth be freed from the curse of human sinfulness? Only through God appointing and anointing a successor to Adam to have 'authority *on earth* to forgive sins'. This is clearly how Luke saw Jesus. This Jesus who is 'the Son of

Man [who] has authority on earth to forgive sins' undoes the earth-damaging work of Adam. Luke is in no doubt that the person and work of Jesus are related to the first Adam. He may not articulate it with the eloquence of Paul in Romans 5 and 1 Corinthians 15. Yet two chapters earlier, in the climax of his genealogy of Jesus, Luke unequivocally states that this Son of Man who has authority on earth to forgive sins in chapter 5 is descended directly from none other than the 'Son of Adam', i.e. 'Son of the one hewn from the earth'. 'Jesus was about thirty years old when he began his *work*. He was the son of Joseph . . . son of Enos, son of Seth, son of Adam, son of God' (Luke 3.23–38).

In the heart of the earth

Let us turn to Matthew for the second time that the Son of Man and the earth appear in the same context.

Forgiveness presupposes judgement. The authority of the Son of Man to forgive sins on earth assumes that the earth and its people are under some form of divine judgement. This is a theological idea which is out of fashion in many church circles, although it is bedded in the imagination of popular attitudes with the question, 'Well, if there is a God, why doesn't he do something about the state of the world?' There is an expectation that God will discern between good and bad, divide the people and act against those and that which is evil. Herein lies an aspiration for a God of justice to judge! I have often said that if we press the question and the hope for God to act in such a way, who, do we imagine, would be left? Such a longing for justice leaves us hoping for mercy. We look to God therefore to be both Judge and Saviour.

This notion that the earth and its people live under some experience of judgement is strongly felt by environmental lobbyists who daily point to the result of abusive human exploitation of the planet and to the ecological crisis now upon us. Crisis is the Greek word for judgement. When the media broadcast the headline 'Environmental Crisis' they are declaring to the world a truth greater than we realize. We are reaping what we sow. This is the crisis, the judgement: 'Do not be deceived,' wrote Paul, 'God is not mocked, for you reap whatever you sow' (Galatians 6.7).

It is in the context of judgement that we come to our next passage in which we find Jesus speaking of himself as 'Son of Man' and in the same breath talking about the earth (Matthew 12.40 ff.). 'For just as Jonah was three days and three nights in the belly of a sea monster, so for three days and three nights the Son of Man will be in the heart of the earth.' This reference to his death and burial yields many possible comparisons with Jonah's experience. For the purpose of this book I confine myself to the significance of laying the Son of Man, Son of Adam, 'in the heart of the earth' by simply posing the question, 'What happened to the earth when he died?' The earth quaked (Matthew 27.51). What happened when God raised him from the earth? The earth quaked again (Matthew 28.2). Prior to placing him in the earth and when raising him from the earth there were great earthquakes.

I have to confess that when preaching about the crucifixion I have seldom spoken of the earthquake, preferring to concentrate on that other phenomenon, the tearing of the temple curtain from top to bottom.

I have overlooked that in the Passion narrative the earth speaks as powerfully as the curtain. As the Son of the one hewn from the earth is laid in the heart of the earth there is a seismic response from the earth's heart to his death and resurrection. Is this a voice in the chorus of the collective groaning of the whole of creation which Paul writes about in Romans 8.22? The earth, God's creation, is longing for liberation from the curse in Genesis and somehow knows that its own freedom 'from the bondage of decay' is inextricably bound up with 'the children of God' and 'their redemption' and 'their freedom', and that comes about through the death and resurrection of Christ Jesus 'who has set us free' and in whom there is 'now no condemnation' (Romans 8).

Staying with the motif of judgement, it cannot escape consideration that Jonah's sojourn in the belly of a whale was a direct result of his disobedience and his determination 'to flee from the presence of the Lord' (Jonah 1.9). Like Adam with Eve who first 'hid themselves from the presence of the Lord' (Genesis 3.9) after the fateful act of disobedience when they ate of the tree in the middle of the Garden of Eden, so Jonah found himself under the judgement of God. The judgement on Adam was to 'return to the earth, and to the dust you shall return' (Genesis 3.19). When, therefore, Jesus says that the Son of Adam will, like Jonah judged in the belly of a whale, be laid in the heart of the earth, are there echoes here of the judgement of the first Adam who was sentenced to return to the earth? The second Adam, the Son of Man, retraces the steps of the first Adam and tastes vicariously the wages of sin – not just death, exclusion from the presence of God, but the return to earth from whence the human family came. The question is therefore raised: As the Son of Man is laid in the heart of the earth after the manner of Adam and Jonah, is there a hint here of God's judgement being visited on Jesus vicariously as he takes upon himself the sins of the cosmos that desecrate the earth? Whatever construction is to be put on the story, the truth is that the earth did not stay silent as it witnessed the Son of Man's death and resurrection.

There are two other instances of earthquakes in the Gospel of Matthew. The first is in the catalogue of cataclysmic events that will preface 'the birthpangs' of the end of the age (Matthew 24.3, 8). 'For nation will rise against nation, and kingdom against kingdom, and there will be famines and earthquakes in various places: all this is but the beginning of the birthpangs' (Matthew 24.7, 8).

The language of labour pains in the Gospel here is of a piece with the word and image that Paul used in Romans 8.22 of the whole of creation being in labour. The earth quakes as the whole of creation goes into labour to give birth to the reality of the new earth and the new heavens as prophesied in Isaiah 65. Central to these eschatological events on earth according to Jesus in the same chapter in Matthew is none other than 'the Son of Man' (Matthew 24.27–31). Without going into the detail of this apocalyptic passage the point to make is that Jesus, the Son of Man, seems especially conscious of his relationship with the earth, and the earth seems vigorously vocal as the mission of the Son of Man unfolds. Indeed, in Matthew 19.28 Jesus sees the 'Son of Man' as central to 'the renewal of all things'. The word for renewal here is *palingenesis* – 'the birth again' of all things. Jesus said to them,

'Truly I tell you, at the renewal of all things, when the Son of Man is seated on the throne of Glory you who have followed me . . . will inherit eternal life.'

The fourth and first earthquake in Matthew's Gospel is hidden from view by the way it is translated. It is in Matthew 8 (the four earthquakes in Matthew's Gospel are in 8.23–7, 24.7–8, 27.51–4 and 28.2). Jesus has spoken poignantly of how he, the Son of Man, has nowhere to lay his head. The foxes have holes (in the earth) and the birds of heaven their nests, but he is pillowless. Getting into a boat on the Sea of Galilee he falls asleep. And there is a storm; actually it's more than a storm – it's an earthquake. In Greek the word here is *seismos*. This is what accounts for the boat being swamped by a great wave. When Jesus then silences the sea and the wind the disciples were amazed and begged the question, 'What sort of person is this?' The earth that gave birth to Adam now raises the question as to the identity of Jesus, the Son of Adam, at the outset of his mission. And what is that mission? To do God's will on earth as it is done in heaven. It is his prayer and ours. His mission and ours. The earthing of heaven. This is the mission of God. Little wonder the earth quakes as that mission unfolds through the unique ministry of the Son of Adam.

Lifted up from the earth

Turning to the Gospel of John we are arrested by the declaration: 'All things came into being through him, and without him not one thing came into being.' This is a confessional statement about the Word who is Jesus. This is echoed through the primary chapters of

Colossians, Ephesians and Hebrews. Colossians 1.16: 'For in him all things in heaven and on earth were created, things visible and invisible . . . all things have been created through him and for him.' Never has so much theology hung on two such small prepositions, 'through' and 'for'!

It is these credal statements that lead to a high view of creation. It is the gift of Christ. Respect for and reverence of the earth follows as it does for the whole of the created order contained in that small 'all'. This distinctively Christian insight ought to shape and form a Christian's attitude to the environment. Creation does not exist for the human family but for Christ. The earth is here for us to delight in, to manage, to serve, but its centre is inhabited by Christ alone and not us. It is a blasphemy to usurp Christ's place. When critics of Christian attitudes to the environment such as the ecologist Lyn White have lambasted us for elevating ourselves over the rest of creation and exploiting it by our own devices and for our own desires they have been right to challenge such anthropocentrism. The Bible dethrones such ambitions and affirms the centrality of Christ not just to salvation but also to creation.

In John 12 we find a third Son of Man/earth saying: '"And I, when I am lifted up from the earth, will draw all people [all things] to myself." He said this to indicate the kind of death he was to die. The crowd answered . . . "How can you say the Son of Man must be lifted up?"' Here again the Son of Man is found in the same context as the earth and is cast in the role of the one who will draw all to himself. Echoes again of Colossians: 'And through him God was pleased to reconcile to himself all things, whether on earth or in heaven by making peace through the blood of his cross.' The Son of Man's ministry is one of connectedness with the earth. Jesus self-consciously sees himself on a mission through which he should lose nothing of what has been given to him. 'I have come down from heaven [to earth] not to do my own will, but the will of him who sent me. And this is the will of him who sent me, that I should lose nothing of all that he has given me' (John 6.39). Jesus has the whole cosmos in his sights, not just individual souls who want to escape earth and bag a place elsewhere. The earth is within God's cosmic purposes.

The earth as God's footstool

Jesus had a high view of the earth even though he fully recognized that it was blighted by the curse of human sinfulness. In Matthew 5 he tells his followers, 'But I say to you, do not swear at all, either by heaven, for it is the throne of God, or by the earth, for it is his footstool.' The latter image might suggest something demeaning, a picture of God Atlas-like with fist on forehead, knee bent and trampling earth beneath his foot. Nothing could be further from the truth. 'Footstool' was far from a demeaning image; it was the word used to describe the Ark of the Covenant. 'I had planned to build a house of rest for the Ark of the Covenant of the Lord, for the footstool of our God' (1 Chronicles 28.2). The footstool is God's touching place, where his presence is found. Isaiah says:

Heaven is my throne
and the earth is my footstool . . .
. . . all these things my hand has made
And so all these things are mine. (Isaiah 66.1, 2)

Herein lies the sacredness of the earth and the theological truth upon which Christians form an ethic about the earth. The reason we respect and cherish the earth is precisely because it is God's footstool, his resting place. This comes through again in Jesus' understanding in Matthew 10.29. 'Are not two sparrows sold for a penny? Yet not one of them falls to the earth apart from your Father.' This verse shows the universal care of God. In many translations 'knowledge', 'knowing' or 'will' are added to 'Father'. But in the original it is simply 'without your Father'. Jesus shows God connected with the earth, Emmanuel, God with us.

Even though the earth is cursed by human sinfulness and bears all the wounds of exploitation and abuse it is nevertheless originally good and graced by the presence of God. So what is the future of the earth? The New Testament uses ambiguous language when painting pictures of the earth's future, language of continuity and discontinuity as we shall see in Chapter 3. I side with those who believe that there will be a continuity between the earth as we now know it 'and the new heaven and the new earth' featured in Isaiah 65 and Revelation. The vivid language used to describe the future and in particular the return of Christ suggests for the future a time of crisis as the earth gives birth to a new and transformed earth.

The mission of the Son of Man is the renewing of all things. Jesus comes to the earth as the Son of Man urging us to pray for the coming of God's Kingdom which is the doing of God's will on earth as it is done in heaven. As we shall see later in this book, the implications of the prayer are personal, parochial and political. Whatever the relationship is between the

Son of Man and the earth the clear message of the Gospels is that the earth is the arena of the mission of Jesus. Some may think that I have made too much of the passages where Jesus speaks of himself of the Son of Man and in the same breath talks of the earth.

Meanwhile I conclude this first chapter reflecting on how we actually pray the Lord's Prayer liturgically. It expresses and reinforces the Church's disconnectedness from the earth.

> Our Father (Pause)
> who art in heaven (Pause)
> hallowed be thy name (Pause)
> thy Kingdom come (Pause)
> thy will be done (Pause)
> on earth as it is in heaven (Pause . . .)

We abstract and dislocate the doing of God's will from the sphere of the incarnation! Admittedly, there is a comma in the Greek text yet the petition that parallels the yearning for the coming Kingdom is 'Thy will be done on earth as it is in Heaven'. Admittedly too we need to take a breath, but we would do better to breathe after the earth than before it!

The consummation of the coming Kingdom is the earthing of heaven. World mission is the earthing of heaven globally. Local mission is the earthing of heaven locally. The sooner we leave out the pause between 'thy will be done' and 'on earth as it is in heaven' the greater will be our own connection with the earth and the deeper will be our obedience to the commitment of Jesus to the earth, present and future.

Discussion

Questions for further reflection on your own or with others.

1 *How worried are you about the future of the earth? Put yourself on this scale:*

   0   1   2   3   4   5   6   7   8   9   10
   Not worried   *Extremely*
   at all   *worried*

   What reasons would you give for this anxiety?

2 *To what extent should we do something about the planet's future? Put yourself on this scale:*

   0   1   2   3   4   5   6   7   8   9   10
   Don't bother   *Absolutely*
                                       imperative

3 *Hopkins says 'Nature is never spent'. Can and how would you justify such optimism?*

4 *Hopkins adds, 'there lives the dearest freshness deep down things'. To what is he alluding?*

5 *Hopkins writes of the Holy Ghost brooding over the bent world 'With warm breast and with ah! bright wings.' What is the role of the Holy Spirit in creation?*

6 *Where would you look in the Bible for guidance about how we should care for the earth?*

7 *What examples could you give of an environmental crisis evidencing the principle of reaping what you sow?*

8 *What examples would you give of repentance on the part of human beings affecting the earth?*

9 *The earthquake at the crucifixion and the resurrection:*

Then Jesus cried again with a loud voice and breathed his last.

At that moment the curtain of the temple was torn in two, from top to bottom. The earth shook, and the rocks were split. The tombs were also opened, and many bodies of the saints who had fallen asleep were raised. After his resurrection they came out of the tombs and entered the holy city and appeared to many. Now when the centurion and those with him, who were keeping watch over Jesus, saw the earthquake and what took place, they were terrified and said, 'Truly this man was God's Son!'

Many women were also there, looking on from a distance; they had followed Jesus from Galilee and had provided for him. Among them were Mary Magdalene, and Mary the mother of James and Joseph, and the mother of the sons of Zebedee.

When it was evening, there came a rich man from Arimathea, named Joseph, who was also a disciple of Jesus. He went to Pilate and asked for the body of Jesus; then Pilate ordered it to be given to him. So Joseph took the body and wrapped it in a clean linen cloth and laid it in his own new tomb, which he had hewn in the rock. He then rolled a great stone to the door of the tomb and went away. Mary Magdalene and the other Mary were there, sitting opposite the tomb.

The next day, that is, after the day of Preparation, the chief priests and the Pharisees gathered before Pilate and said, 'Sir, we remember what that impostor said while he was still alive. "After three days I will rise again." Therefore command that the tomb be made secure until the third day: otherwise his disciples may go and steal him away, and tell the people, "He has been raised from the dead", and the last deception would be worse than the first.' Pilate said to them, 'You have a guard of soldiers; go, make it as secure as you can.' So they went with the guard and made the tomb secure by sealing the stone.

After the sabbath, as the first day of the week was dawning, Mary Magdalene and the other Mary went to see the tomb. And suddenly there was a great earthquake; for an angel of the Lord, descending from heaven, came and rolled back the stone and sat on it. His appearance was like lightning, and his clothing white as snow. For fear of him the guards shook and became like dead men. But the angel said to the women, 'Do not be afraid; I know that you are looking for Jesus who was crucified. He is not here; for he has been raised, as he said. Come, see the place where he lay. Then go quickly and tell his disciples, "He has been raised from the dead, and indeed he is going ahead of you to Galilee; there you will see him". This is my message for you.'

Reflect on this passage and imagine how it would read without the two earthquakes.

10 *'Thy will be done on earth as it is in heaven.'*
Meditate on this prayer. Repeat it prayerfully
frequently. At the end, note the pictures that came
to mind.

Chapter 2

The Son of Man Came Eating and Drinking

Natural consumers

Christianity is a religion of consumption. We are natural and original consumers. The Garden of Eden is planted with food for us to eat. And when the founder of Christianity departed this life he gave his followers an act of consumption by which to remember him. Taking and breaking bread during the Passover meal, Jesus identified it as his body, and the wine as his blood, and then called on his followers to eat and drink in remembrance of him. So misunderstood was this act of consumption that some early critics of Christianity accused Christians of cannibalism!

I open this chapter with this salvo because in a world where many over-indulge, some Christians can easily over-react by denying any virtue in consumption. The history of heresy in Christianity is when someone discovers an omission then compensates by over-emphasizing the corrective so that the pendulum swings again in the opposite, heretical direction. It is true that it was through an act of consumption, the disobedient eating of an apple, that sin entered into the world, but equally it is through an act of consumption that the world is also redeemed. As George

25

Herbert expressed it so beautifully to the unkind and ungrateful one whose eyes are so shamefully marred: 'You must sit down, says Love, and taste my meat: So I did sit and eat.' It is through consuming these holy mysteries that the soul which drew back guilty of dust and sin finds Love's welcome. Consumption therefore is not essentially sinful. It has the potential to redeem.

Love bade me welcome: yet my soul drew back,
    Guilty of dust and sin.
But quick-ey'd Love, observing me grow slack
    From my first entrance in,
Drew nearer to me, sweetly questioning,
    If I lack'd any thing.

A guest, I answer'd, worthy to be here:
    Love said, you shall be he.
I the unkind, ungrateful? Ah my dear,
    I cannot look on thee.
Love took my hand, and smiling did reply,
    Who made the eyes but I?

Truth Lord, but I have marr'd them: let my shame
    Go where it doth deserve.
And know you not, says Love, who bore the
    blame?
My dear, then I will serve.
You must sit down, says Love, and taste my meat:
    So I did sit and eat.

If this thought that there is virtue in consuming seems incredible, it would not be the first time that religious people remained unconvinced of the merits of consumption. You will remember that when 'the Son of

Man came eating and drinking' his enemies were so outraged by his lifestyle that they accused Jesus of being a glutton and drunkard. They compared him with his ascetic cousin John the Baptist who 'came neither eating nor drinking' and made the comparison in order to belittle Jesus (Matthew 11.18, 19).

The history of Christianity has been blighted by those who have denied the essential materialism of creation and the gospel. It was William Temple who insisted that Christianity was the most material of all the religions. Genesis opens with the declaration that the whole of God's material creation is good. A cursory glance at the Gospels shows that Jesus' was a material ministry serving people's physical needs. The resurrection of the body of Jesus is central to the Christian faith not just because of the veracity of the scriptures but because, as John Polkinghorne has said, 'matter matters to God'. Indeed, to the Jewish mind with its holistic attitude to creation, in stark contrast to the dualism of Hellenistic philosophical systems, there was no resurrection conceivable that did not include the body. In the new dispensation of the future Paul looks forward not to a world of disembodied spirits but to 'the redemption of our body'.

There is a continuum between the opening chapters of Genesis with its emphasis on the original goodness of the material world and the resurrection of the body of Jesus which declares that the material has a place in the eternal purpose of God.

The central petition of the Lord's Prayer seeks the doing of God's will on earth as it is in heaven. This plea for the earthing of heaven is followed logically by the asking for the provision of daily bread. However much the Church, unable to shrug off completely the cloak of the Manichean heresy, of elevating the spiritual over the physical, has sought down the years to spiritualize and dematerialize this prayer, the fact is that Jesus Christ, the earthy revelation of God, exercises a material ministry. Jesus, the Son of Man, like his earthy ancestor Adam, came into the world 'eating and drinking'.

Even if these acts of consumption were deemed selfish activities it needs to be said that not everything that is selfish is necessarily sinful. Breathing is essentially selfish but it is not deemed unethical. Eating and drinking can, of course, become the means of excessive self-indulgence and often do. But although they are essentially self-centred they are not essentially sinful. Jesus, by comparison with his cousin John, is clearly identified as a consumer, the material human being. The Son of Man is the earthy expression of the Word becoming flesh.

But to draw attention to the consuming Christ puts us on a collision course with those who feel that Christianity, especially in the West, has already and too readily sanctioned and sanctified consumerism and global greed. Many green ethicists have laid the blame for the West's exploitation of the earth's resources at the biblical door of Christianity. They feel that the verses which have given *carte blanche* to humankind to exploit the earth are Genesis 1.28 and 29:

God blessed them, and God said to them, 'Be fruitful and multiply, and fill the earth and subdue it; and have dominion over the fish of the sea and over the birds of the air and over every living thing that moves upon the earth.' God said, 'See, I have

given you every plant yielding seed that is upon
the face of all the earth, and every tree with seed in
its fruit; you shall have them for food.'

Genesis certainly portrays humankind as natural
consumers and born traders. The sense of the word
'dominion' is strong and, left unqualified, could
indeed support the view that human beings are mon-
archs of all they survey. But the position of the human
family in the world is soon qualified in the following
chapter where God explicitly charges the gardener of
Eden 'to till it and keep it'. The word 'till' has it roots
in the Hebrew word 'to serve'. Adam who is hewn
from the earth is called to serve the very earth from
which he was formed. He is a part of the creation and
not apart from it. The apex of creation is not
humankind: it is Christ through whom all things came
into being and for whom all exists. Christ, the Son of
Adam, is the curb on human vanity and our greedy
ambitions. All is ultimately for him and not for us.

In Alastair's McIntosh's inspiring book *Soil and
Soul* he tells the story of a multinational company
determined to turn a Hebridean island into a gravel
pit. The islanders are torn between their need of jobs
and their love of the land. The issue comes to a Public
Inquiry and those resisting the advances of the multi-
national enlist as witnesses two unlikely bedfellows –
Stone Eagle, a Canadian First Nations chieftain, and
Professor Donald Macleod, Principal of the Free
Church of Scotland College. His testimony to the
Public Inquiry is a cogent exposition of Genesis and is
worth reprinting in full:

1   God as Creator has absolute sovereignty over the environment. We must use it only in accordance with His will; and we shall answer, collectively as well as individually, for all our decisions in this area.

2   Theologically, the primary function of the Creation is to serve as a revelation of God. To spoil the Creation is to disable it from performing this function.

3   In the Judaeo–Christian tradition there is an intimate link between man and the soil. He is taken from the ground; his food is derived from it; he is commanded to till and keep it; and he returns to it. This implies a psychological as well as theological bond. Although such facts should not be used to endorse naked territorialism, they do raise the consideration that rape of the environment is rape of the community itself.

4.   The precise responsibility of man to his environment is defined very precisely in the Judaeo–Christian tradition.

4.1 Man has to 'keep' it (Genesis 2.15). This is not simply an insistence on conservation. It designates man as guardian and protector of the ground.

4.2 Man is the *servant* of the ground (Genesis 2.15). This is the usual meaning of the Hebrew word popularly rendered to us as *to till*. Christian theology has largely failed to recognize this emphasis. Any insistence on the more widely perceived notion of man's *dominion* (Genesis 1.28) must be balanced by the less familiar but equally important concept of man as servant.

5   There is no place in the Judaeo-Christian
     tradition for divided guardianship of the land.
     In particular, there is no place for the idea that
     agrarian rights may belong to the people,
     while mineral rights belong to someone else.
     This dichotomy is central to the current
     debate. From a theological point of view, the
     present arrangements, while perfectly legal, are
     indefensible.

6   Man's relationship with his environment has
     been disrupted by the Fall. One primary
     symptom of this is that he is always tempted
     to allow economic considerations to override
     ecological ones. In the present instance the
     divinely appointed guardians and servants of
     Lingerabay are the people of Harris. Unfortu-
     nately, these very people are now suffering a
     degree of economic hardship that threatens the
     very survival of their community. Torn
     between their love for the land and their need
     for jobs, they face a cruel dilemma. Capitalism
     offers to help them in characteristic fashion:
     it will relieve unemployment provided the
     people surrender guardianship of the land
     (thus violating their own deepest instincts).

     The people of Harris live conscious of the
     glory of God. What I'm asking is to reflect on
     whether this project is to the glory of God. Do
     we have God's mandate to inflict on Creation
     a scar of this magnitude that might detract
     from Creation's ability to reflect the glory of
     God? I know that Roineabhal is not in itself
     an area of what you might deem to be 'beauti-
     ful'. It is nevertheless an area of magnificence

31

and grandeur and, by being such, bears
eloquent testimony in my judgement to
the majesty and grandeur of God's Earth.
In my view no hole in the ground could bear
that testimony as Roineabhal presently does.
(Presented by Alastair McIntosh for Donald
Macleod at Leverburgh, Isle of Harris, 1994)

A radical Presbyterian (which given the image of the
'Wee Frees' may seem a contradiction), he is credited
for having said that 'Adam was a crofter and only the
Fall gave us landlords' and that the Sabbath was given
as an 'employment protection measure'. His summary
of the Christian attitude to the environment recognizes the needs of the community at the same time as
circumscribing it with responsibilities for the earth.

Discerning consumers

'Out of the earth the Lord God made to grow every
tree that is pleasant to the sight and good for food.'
God makes provision for our needs with extravagant
and open-handed generosity. Aesthetic and culinary
delights are generously provided for our consumption. But they are gifts for and not goals of our
existence. They, like the land, belong to God. There
are boundaries, limits to our consumption. According
to the Chief Rabbi the forbidden 'Tree of the knowledge of good and evil' stands there as an inhibition, to
circumscribe human freedom, to put and to keep the
human family in its place. Everything does *not* exist
for humankind. That is an arrogance. The Tree stands
in the same way as the Sabbath and Jubilee Festivals.
The Sabbath and Jubilee laws in Leviticus which

govern the use of the earth make it abundantly clear that whereas God delights in our enjoyment of the fruit of the earth, 'The land shall not be sold in perpetuity.' Why? 'For the land is mine, with me you are but aliens and tenants.' We are born natural consumers, but from the outset there are to be limits to our consumption.

Interestingly and maybe surprisingly it was Lady Thatcher who early in her premiership argued that when it came to the planet we were but tenants with a full repairing lease and with a duty to hand it on to future generations in as good a condition as we found it. The same point is made by the African proverb, 'We have borrowed the present from our children.'

The Bible envisages humanity as discerning, responsible and ethical consumers who are called to ensure fair shares and justice for the widow, the orphan, the asylum seeker, the disadvantaged, the voiceless, the lame, the least, the last and the lost. The Bible recognizes the reality of sin and the need for repentance in order to create a society of justice and mercy.

The gospel has an earthy feel to it. The Nazareth manifesto in Luke 4 cannot be dematerialized and spiritualized. Jesus' own examples of healing the sick and feeding the hungry explicitly tell of his mission to help people materially and physically, and his startling prophecy that those who had fed the hungry and clothed the destitute will find that they have done it to him personally should leave us in no doubt of the moral imperative to act materially and to rescue the poor.

The earth is a rich storehouse of food. Only one thing stands in the way of all being able to consume what they need, and this is injustice. The most compelling argument for developing genetically modified foods is that they might eradicate world hunger. Yet there is already materially enough food for all to be fed. It is a striving for justice rather than a high-risk and no-turning-back experimenting with technology that will rectify the imbalance between rich and poor. My fear with genetically modified processes is that they will ultimately serve the purposes and the profits of the transnational GM companies rather than the poor and will eliminate the hungry rather than hunger. The doing of God's will on earth as it is done in heaven requires us to challenge unjust structures, political and economic, and to insist on fair trade and sustainable methods of food and fuel production. The earthing of heaven requires it.

A new earth?

Yet many Christians still sit loose to this understanding of the gospel, preferring to see the priority in saving souls for heaven. But the biblical hope for the future involves a new heaven *and* a new earth. Just as there is a continuum between the bodies we now inhabit and our spiritual bodies in the future, so there will be a continuity between this earth and the new earth. The Kingdom that Jesus inaugurates is the one where heaven finally comes down to earth. It is the earthing of heaven in a new heaven and a transformed earth that consummates the central petition of the Kingdom Prayer – the coming of the Kingdom through the doing on earth of God's will as it is done in heaven.

Living together in such harmony is the stuff of songwriters. John Lennon sang 'Give peace a chance' and Bono pleads: 'Heaven on earth, We need it now'. It is like the song that the angels sang to those startled shepherds on the hills outside Bethlehem:

Glory to God in the highest Heaven
And Peace on Earth.

The shepherds lived a hard life in the open air. Day and night they watched over their sheep and guarded the lambs from ravenous wolves. If you could have asked them what peace on earth or heaven on earth would have looked like, they would probably have said, 'A world where you didn't have to live out in the fields in the depth of winter, and at the dead of night looking after sheep and protecting young lambs from ravenous wolves.' Their ideal world, their idea of a new and heavenly earth, would have been where 'the wolf and the lamb lie down and feed together'. And, of course, that's exactly the picture of heaven on earth that God gave to the prophet Isaiah. He said:

I am about to create new heavens
And a new earth . . .
Where the wolf and the lamb shall feed together.
(Isaiah 65.17, 25)

That's a powerful picture of harmony where the animals stop feeding off each other and instead feed together.

The angel told the shepherds that the one who would bring about this heavenly and harmonious world was about to be born in Bethlehem. The angels called him 'a Saviour'. The sign of this Saviour and of the new world that he would bring about would be – and this must have shocked the shepherds who knew all about animals – the baby lying in an animal feeding trough! What? Who would ever put a newborn baby in a trough where the donkey, goat and dog munch their food? The baby wouldn't have been safe! Except that this baby was different. He was anointed, special and the Saviour. This unique baby lying in a manger, in a feeding trough, was a sign of how the Saviour was bringing about a new harmony on earth – a harmony not just between the wolf and lamb but between the human family and the animal kingdom. And he wouldn't stop there. Peace on earth would mean the breaking down of all barriers between people.

This peace on earth comes through God entering into the world and through Jesus the Son of Man walking the face of the earth with the talk of God's love, and especially with his authority to forgive. From the womb to the tomb, one of us. From the cradle to the grave, the Saviour. On the cross he forgives and saves us from our sins and blesses us with peace – with God and with each other. Paul wrote about it powerfully in Ephesians 2.13–18:

> But now in Christ Jesus you who once were far off have been brought near by the blood of Christ. For he is our peace; in his flesh he has made both groups into one and has broken down the dividing wall, that is, the hostility between us. He has abolished the law with its commandments and ordinances, so that he might create in himself one new humanity in place of the two, thus making peace, and might reconcile both groups to God in one body through the cross, thus putting to death that hostility through it. So he came and proclaimed peace to you who were far off and peace to those who were near; for through him both of us have access in one Spirit to the Father.

Through his death, Jesus breaks down the barrier between us and God and so breaks down the dividing wall between the different tribes of the human family. This is the route, the road map to peace and to one new humanity.

The earth aches for this peace and yearns for a radical transformation. But the Johannesburg Earth Summit showed that for all the talking, we seem powerless to overcome our self-centredness. Michael Meacher, previously the UK Minister for the Environment, writes: 'There is a lot wrong with our world. But it is not as bad as many people think. It is actually worse.' The earth cries out for peace, especially as the nations of the world line up against nations.

Bono's song goes on:

> Jesus could you take the time
> To throw a drowning man a line
> Peace on earth.

Jesus is central to God's plan for peace on earth.

Escaping the earth?

Some, however, will point to a famous passage about consumption and argue that the thrust of the gospel is surely to escape this earth to find a place in heaven.

> Do not store up for yourselves treasures on earth, where moth and rust consume and where thieves break in and steal; but store up for yourselves treasures in heaven, where neither moth nor rust consumes and where thieves do not break in and

steal. For where your treasure is, there your heart
will be also. (Matthew 6.19 ff.)

The traditional interpretation of this passage is to
curb consumption here on earth in order to invest in
the dividends of an other-worldly heaven. But there
may be another way of understanding it. In all the
translations 'moth' is paralleled with 'rust' but the
word in Greek that goes with rust is actually 'eating'.
Moreover, the word 'consume' does not give the full
force of the activity which actually means to 'make
vanish'. The verses could equally well read, 'Do not
store up for yourselves treasures on earth where
moths and consumption make things vanish but store
up for yourselves treasures in heaven where neither
moths nor consumption make things disappear.'

The contrast is between a world here and now
where material things are consumed and disappear,
they vanish and become extinct, and a new world
where material things are consumed but do not disappear, vanish and become extinct. In other words,
the new world is a realm of sustainable consumption,
or to use a better phrase coined by the Christian
ecologist Edward Echlin, 'sustainable sufficiency' (see
his book *Earth Spirituality*). The new world, for
which the disciples are encouraged to pray earlier in
the chapter, namely heaven earthed, is a realm where
moths and eating/consuming do not make things
extinct. In heaven on earth the material world is
sustained, renewed and not exploited. The consumers
are just and discerning.

Another George Herbert poem called 'Providence'
evokes such a sustainable world:

Bees work for man; and yet they never bruise
Their master's flower, but leave it, having done,
As fair as ever, and as fit to use;
So both the flower doth stay, and honey run.

As Edward Echlin has written, 'sustainability means taking from the earth's resources what is sufficient for today's needs, for all creatures, without compromising the ability of future generations, of all creatures, to live with sustainable sufficiency' (*Earth Spirituality*). It cannot be without significance that if heaven on earth is a realm of sustainable consumption then the picture that Jesus gives us of hell is of unrecyclable waste. Gehenna, his picture of hell, was in the Valley of Hinnom which was the municipal rubbish dump outside Jerusalem. It was a smouldering heap polluting the air, the earth and the water. Such was Jesus' picture of hell, that of an unsustainable tip!

Sustainable sufficiency

How then do we go about establishing a world of sustainable sufficiency where consumers are realistic in their expectations and just in their demands? The African proverb quoted earlier, 'We have borrowed the present from our children' is crammed with the full force of the idea that is known as intergenerational justice. This embraces the notion that ethical behaviour must recognize the rights of future generations, especially in matters of consumption, be it food, fuel or water. However, this ethical position has been challenged by Oxford philosophers Wilfred Beckerman and Joanna Pasek in their book *Justice, Posterity and the Environment*. Their argument is really very simple:

1 Future generations – of unborn people – cannot be said to have any rights.
2 Any coherent theory of justice implies conferring rights on people.
3 The interests of future generations cannot be protected or promoted within the framework of any theory of justice.

They write from a secular, humanist perspective. Their argument is compelling provided you leave God out of the picture and any sense of human accountability to God for the present and future state of the earth. Our connectedness is not just with all creatures in the present but with all creatures in the future. Our actions have consequences both now and in the future. Indeed, the future more than the present reveals the moral quality of our actions. Clearly those who do not exist at this moment in time cannot be said to be possessed of any rights. To have regard for them and their needs derives from the moral demands not of them but of their God and ours who holds in himself the past, the present and the future. Although Beckerman and Pasek challenge the very principles of intergenerational justice as nonsensical they nevertheless believe that the interests of future generations are best served by us seeking justice in our own time. We need to be mindful of justice in the way we consume the earth's resources.

Paul Hawken and Amory Lovins in *Natural Capitalism: Creating the Next Industrial Revolution* accept the realities of the marketplace and the character of human beings as natural consumers and born traders. They advocate four key strategies to 'avert scarcity, perpetuate abundance and provide a solid

basis for social development; it is the basis of responsible stewardship and prosperity for the next century
and beyond'. The four key strategies are:

1 Radical resource productivity which means
   gaining more from products and processes while
   using less material and energy. The development of
   the Hypercar is the classic example of this.
2 Biomimicry means eliminating the idea of waste by
   redesigning industrial processes along biological
   lines. We need to develop processes that mimic biological systems such as chlorophyll turning sunlight
   into energy at no cost to the environment and as the
   spider producing silk as strong as any synthetic
   fabric without needing to boil sulphuric acid!
3 Service and flow means changing the relationship
   between the producer and the consumer. The
   manufacturers should take life-long responsibility
   for their products so that they enter into a service
   agreement with the consumer to repair, improve,
   recycle and redesign the material. The classic
   example would be such household goods as washing
   machines, dishwashers and refrigerators. Instead of
   these being dumped on a tip the manufacturer
   would become deliverers of a service, providing
   long-lasting, upgradeable durables. Rather than an
   economy in which goods are made and sold and
   dumped there would be a service-economy 'where
   consumers would obtain services by leasing or
   renting goods rather than buying them outright'.
4 Investing in natural capital sees re-investment in
   the biosphere as the greatest priority if we are not
   to bankrupt the earth. Our greatest natural
   resource is humanity itself. Hitherto economic

activity has centred on the maximum use of natural resources and the minimum amount of labour. Investing and re-investing in our natural and social capital must involve the reversal of the trend, namely the minimum use of natural resources and the maximum use of labour.

These four strategies do harmonize with a biblical vision of creation and the dignity of humanity. They are not Luddite. They are not based on a false nostalgia. (I like the satirist P. J. O'Rourke's challenge to any who want to go back to the past. He says one word: 'Dentistry'!) Hawken and Lovins recognize the realities of the planet and the moral vision of humankind's responsibility for the earth.

Every year in the UK the British Council of Shopping Centres holds a convention. Recently they invited me to address them on sustainable development and social responsibility. This convention involves some of the biggest retail property owners whose portfolios include the large out-of-town shopping malls and some of the biggest high street retailers. I offered a definition of sustainability as 'enjoying the earth's resources without jeopardizing the welfare of future generations'. I called for realism and idealism. Sustainability without the recognition that we are natural consumers and born traders denies our very humanity. Consumption without sustainability is, however, short-sighted and immoral. I argued that the consumer of the future would be much more environmentally aware.

I strongly suspect that future consumers will be more discerning about what, where and how they buy. I imagine they will be more discerning about the siting and designing of the buildings that they shop in, materials, the source of energy and especially ease of access that does not involve a car to reach them. They will be more discerning about the packaging.

Two of the biggest threats to the future of the planet are the abundance of waste and the scarcity of water. In Britain recently we had the extraordinary scenario of nuclear waste from one of our reactors in the north-west of England being shipped around the world via Japan only to return to be buried in one of the most beautiful parts of the country near the Lake District. It was a symbol of how our society is finding it increasingly difficult to handle the waste that it produces.

The Secretary General of the United Nations has predicted that the next world war will be about water:

> About 70 per cent of the earth is made up of water and less than one per cent is terrestrial fresh water, on which all terrestrial life depends. It is therefore all the more serious when this comparatively small amount of water is polluted. (R. L. Sarkar, *The Bible, Ecology and Environment*)

Michael Meacher has estimated that two million children die in our world every year from drinking contaminated water – twice as many every day as were killed on 11 September.

Young people as they grow up will be more discerning about the processes of production, especially the safety of food and the treatment of animals in the food chain. They will, I suspect, also be more discerning about the means of trade, ensuring that the clothes and the shoes that they buy have been made by people who in turn have been paid a fair wage.

It is difficult and hazardous to predict human behaviour. However, my own engagement with young people, including my own three daughters, encourages me to believe that they are more environmentally aware than their parents. They take to heart dramatic pictures such as an area the size of France being lost to the Amazon rainforest. The trees are the lungs of the earth and such deforestation affects the air that we breathe and the climate we inhabit. Although it is difficult to prove categorically that one thing causes another, nevertheless you cannot escape the conclusion that the earth cannot be abused with impunity.

We are natural consumers and born traders. We are given moral responsibility for the earth and its future. Our consumption is to be set within certain limits. The earth is not ultimately for us to exploit but for Christ, through and for whom all things came into being. Revealed to us as the Son of Man, the son of the one hewn from the earth, he entered the world as one of us 'from the womb to the tomb'. A natural consumer, he came eating and drinking. He gave us an activity by which to remember him and invoke his presence. It was and is an act of consumption – eating and drinking, bread and wine. Imagine around that table of 13 people if only four were allowed to partake and nine were excluded. Such an act of greedy consumption on the part of the four simply would not have been tolerated by the Son of Man who in Matthew 25 chides those who ignore the needs and rights of others to consume.

On Christ's earth the consumption of goods is skewed along bad and unjust lines. One-third of the world indulges in two-thirds of the earth's resources while the majority languishes in poverty and disease. I cannot believe that this is a matter of indifference to Jesus. Nor can I believe that those of us who dare to name and follow him can escape the moral force of the judgement of the Son of Man on all consumers, 'In as much as you did not feed the hungry, give drink to the thirsty, befriend the stranger, clothe the destitute you did not do it to me' (see Matthew 25.31, 42–6). The consumer speaks to all consumers.

Discussion

Questions for further reflection on your own or with others.

1 *'You must sit down, says Love, and taste my meat: So I did sit and eat.' What are the virtues of consumption?*

2 *What are the vices of consumption?*

3 *Jesus 'exercised a material ministry'. What examples would you give of this?*

4 *Review the list of reasons given by Professor Macleod to the Public Inquiry. Rearrange the list in order of priority. What have you put first, and why?*

5 *Read Ephesians 2.13–18. Put in your own words how God creates 'one new humanity'.*

6 *How should we view our relationship to future generations?*

7 *Sustainability is 'enjoying the earth's resources without jeopardizing the welfare of future generations'. How in our personal lifestyles do we practically hold together both joy and jeopardy?*

8 *'We have borrowed the present from our children'. Meditate prayerfully by repeating this consciously in the presence of Jesus.*

Chapter 3

The Son of Man Comes On Clouds

Ambivalence to Creation

The Romantic poet William Wordsworth delighted in creation and observed the balance within nature and the relationship between humanity and the rest of the created order. In his poem 'To a Butterfly' he points up the ambivalence to be found in human attitudes to creation:

> My sister Emmeline and I
> Together chased the butterfly!
> A very hunter did I rush
> Upon the prey: with leaps and springs
> I followed on from brake to bush;
> But she, God love her, feared to brush
> The dust from off its wings.

One child sees the butterfly as a challenge, an object to hunt and capture, and the other reveres it, knowing that even to touch it would be to risk damaging it.

This ambivalence towards the natural world possesses humanity: on the one hand exploiting the earth for all its worth, and on the other gazing in awe at the beauty of its form. These two polarized attitudes of self-indulgence and reverence characterize the attitude of the human family to creation. It might be easier if the two attitudes identified two separate groups. In their extreme expressions they do. But for the most part these two opposite dispositions are to be found in each of us, one moment captivated by the beauty of the earth, the next hell-bent on filling the widening gap between need and greed.

The Christian faith is centred on the one 'through whom and for whom all things come into being'. This means that fear of the future which is stoked up by environmental lobbyists needs to be complemented by respect and reverence for everything that belongs to Christ – including the animal kingdom with whom we share the habitat of the earth.

Edward Echlin puts it this way:

When we question the human place, *our* role and duties within the earth community we discover that, as his image, we are God's responsible representatives *within* the earth community. Far from being vertically above the creatures, as Aristotle, the Stoics, and many Christian writers would have us, we are within the created community. (*The Franciscan*, 15.2, May 2003)

He shows the flaw in humanity elevating itself above and apart from the rest of creation. He points how God displaces the arrogance of humanity when he places Job firmly within creaturehood: 'Where were you when I laid the foundations of the earth?'

The connectedness of the human family with and within the whole of the created order in heaven and on earth is celebrated in Psalm 148:

The Son of Man Comes On Clouds

Praise the LORD!
Praise the LORD from the heavens;
praise him in the heights!
Praise him, all his angels;
praise him, all his host!

Praise him, sun and moon;
praise him, all you shining stars!
Praise him, you highest heavens,
and you waters above the heavens!

Let them praise the name of the LORD,
for he commanded and they were created.
He established them for ever and ever;
he fixed their bounds which cannot be passed.

Praise the LORD from the earth,
you sea monsters and all deeps,
fire and hail, snow and frost,
stormy wind fulfilling his command!

Mountains and all hills,
fruit trees and all cedars!
Wild animals and all cattle,
creeping things and flying birds!

Kings of the earth and all peoples,
princes and all rulers of the earth!
Young men and women alike,
old and young together!

Let them praise the name of the LORD,
for his name alone is exalted;
his glory is above earth and heaven.

He has raised up a horn for his people,
praise for all his faithful,
for the people of Israel who are close to him.
Praise the LORD!

Wordsworth's butterfly gives way to sea monsters, wild animals and all cattle, creeping things and flying birds! Those creatures of the earth are members of the choir with us who sing the praise of God. 'Rulers of the earth' we may be, but our worship will be inadequate and unacceptable to God if we fail to appreciate that the one who 'commanded and they were created' has orchestrated a choral symphony in which there are many parts and without whom the paean of God's praise is diminished. Psalm 148 offers no parts to soloists!

Jesus and the animal kingdom

In our disregard of the fullness of God's creation and our interconnectedness with the whole of the created order, Christians, with a few notable exceptions, have failed to see just how aware Jesus was of the animal world. In Matthew's Gospel alone on 27 separate occasions he introduces us to: locusts and birds and dogs and pigs and wolves and sheep and foxes and snakes and doves and sparrows and vipers and fish and camels and donkeys and colts and hens and chicks and vultures and goats and a cock.

In a rhythm worthy of a song from *Joseph and his Amazing Technicolour Dreamcoat* we find Jesus enlisting animals in his conversations about the Kingdom of God.

Jesus was, of course, born in a typical Middle

Eastern house. Contrary to all the Christmas card scenes it was perfectly natural for an extended family to share their dwelling with their animals. It was suggestive of the harmony in the Garden of Eden where before the fatal act of consumption human beings shared the garden with animals. Like every other ordinary child, Jesus lived a life that was connected to the environment, to the animals and to the land. That's why his thoughts are shot through with images of the earth and a variety of God's creatures. In his book *Earth Spirituality: Jesus at the Centre* Edward Echlin shows how connected Jesus was within his own culture to the earth.

Animals tell the good news

Jesus enlists the animals as fellow evangelists. They tell us of God's providence, presence and peace. Jesus says:

> Look at the birds of the air; they neither sow nor reap nor gather into barns, and yet your heavenly Father feeds them. Are you not of more value than they? And can any of you by worrying add a single hour to your span of life? (Matthew 6.26–7)

The birds of heaven are the evangelists to the earth who sing the good news of God's providence: 'If he feeds us he will feed you.' God is the source of sustainable sufficiency and humanity the obstacle to it and the doubter of it. The birds by their very being challenge our doubts and kindle our faith in the generosity of his provision.

If the birds tell us of divine providence and how the blessings of heaven are showered upon the earth, then it is the birds again who sing of God's presence with us, especially in times of tragedy. The human family may doubt that presence and even rebel against it, but Jesus assures us of God's commitment to and connectedness with every aspect of his creation.

> Do not fear those who kill the body but cannot kill the soul; rather fear him who can destroy both soul and body in hell. Are not two sparrows sold for a penny? Yet not one of them will fall to the ground apart from your Father. (Matthew 10.28–9)

The birds of heaven are the evangelists announcing to all the world that not one of them falls to the earth without the Father. Here is the good news: not that we shall be free from enemies – Jesus had plenty – but that when we fall to the ground we are not alone. The good Father is with us. Why? Because the earth is his footstool, his resting place.

Mark in his Gospel says of Jesus: 'He was in the wilderness forty days, tempted by Satan; and he was with the wild beasts; and the angels waited on him' (Mark 1.13). According to Richard Bauckham in his paper 'Jesus and the Animals' the way Mark describes this speaks of 'a sense of close association or friendship'. Here is 'Jesus enjoying the peaceable harmony with wild animals which had been God's original intention.'

At the outset of his ministry it is as if Jesus brings the Garden of Eden into the desert and enlists the wild animals as fellow evangelists of God's peace heralding the Kingdom of Shalom that is to come where 'the wolf shall live with the lamb, and the leopard shall lie down with the kid' (Isaiah 11.6). Here are even the wild animals testifying alongside the domestic animals surrounding the Bethlehem manger to the harmony of the new world that is coming as God brings peace to the new earth.

Animals tell the bad news

As well as being heralds of good news the animals are also enlisted by God as tellers of bad news. When Peter betrays Jesus hot on the heels of the treason of Judas, the cock crows as promised. It is given to a bird to expose the betrayal that in God's over-ruling leads to the salvation of the cosmos. No human being raises any voice to protest on behalf of the Innocent against the betrayal by one of his closest friends. Only a bird whose echoing crow haunted the soul of Peter lifts up his voice in defiant tones against betrayal.

Some would hold – and I for one – that our treatment of the earth and of many of God's creatures amounts to a betrayal of our God-given task to serve the earth and to care and therefore protect the animal world with whom we share the planet. Yet where are the voices to speak out against the denial, this betrayal? Only the cock crows. I heard a sound like it the other day when caught behind a lorry of crates. What was in them was moving, just. And a muffled sound from a living creature was drowned by an engine belching fumes of oil. Only the cock crowed. The image of the cock, free to roam, forage and fill the landscape with its dawn chorus, is a far cry from the way in which poultry is treated in Britain today: 95 per cent of all chickens are destined to live only seven weeks of their seven-year lifespan. What's more, they live life in conditions conveniently hidden behind closed doors which, if seen, heard and smelt, would make vegetarians of us all. The cruelty to which these animals are subjected does not sit comfortably alongside pretensions to be a civilized, let alone a Christian society. It is a very far cry from Wordsworth's Emmeline who for Godly fear and reverence of creation dared not 'brush the dust from off its wings'. One can only imagine the offence given to the Holy Spirit who in the poetic words of Gerard Manley Hopkins broods over the bent world 'with warm breast and with ah! bright wings'.

Human actions and processes of nature

Respect for God's creatures, for the earth and for the whole of creation is, or ought to be, a hallmark of biblical faith. If a hair cannot avoid the attention of God and if a fallen sparrow cannot escape the presence of the good Father then a scudding cloud, presaging a devastating change in climate, cannot be a matter of indifference to God and his people. To this end more than 70 leading scientists, policy-makers and Christian leaders from across six continents gathered for 'Climate Forum 2002' in Oxford, England, to address the growing crisis of human-induced climate change. The Forum recognized the reality and the urgency of the problem, which particularly affects the world's poorest people and the very fabric of the biosphere. The Forum also recognized that the Christian community has a special obligation to provide moral leadership and an example of caring service to people and to all God's creation.

An Indian theologian, R. L. Sarkar, sets the scene in a compelling way in *The Bible, Ecology and Environment*:

All life on Earth is part of one great, interdependent system. It interacts with, and depends on, the non-living components of the planet: atmosphere, oceans, freshwaters, rocks and soils. Humanity depends totally on this community of life – this biosphere – of which we are an integral part.

In the remote past, human actions were trivial when set against the dominant processes of nature. No longer is this so. The human species now influences the fundamental processes of the planet. Ozone depletion, worldwide pollution, and climate change are testimonies to our power.

Sarkar's telling point is that in the past even our mightiest actions were of little consequence by comparison with the great forces of nature. It is this shift in balance that presents us with our predicament today. The power at our disposal and the scale of our activities now dwarf some of the mightiest forces of nature. We have the power even to change the climate of the planet.

At the conference I was asked to give a theological perspective and took as my theme the image of the Son of Man coming on clouds. The vision in the Gospels of the Son of Man coming on clouds is both apocalyptic and eschatological. The changes in climate present apocalyptic and eschatological questions, namely, what is being revealed about the state of the world through climate change and what will the future hold? In other words, what on earth is going on and what will happen to the earth? These questions can be answered scientifically and theologically. These need not be mutually exclusive. Although science is an empirical process, no scientists are free from bringing their own values and philosophical presuppositions to bear on their research. Furthermore, theology cannot be detached from the culture in which its own reflections are being shaped.

When Jesus self-consciously spoke about his own destiny as the Son of Man he was revealing both his present and future roles in the unfolding drama of God's plan for the whole cosmos. The Son of Man on the clouds is a dramatic picture echoing the imagery of the book of Daniel and turns our attention to the future of the world.

These kaleidoscopic images and the very meaning of the title Son of Man are, as we have noted, open to a wide range of interpretations. Theologians do not usually hesitate to go down paths that angels fear to tread, and to the writing of books on the apocalypse and eschatology there is no end!

It seems clear to me that the beliefs that a person holds about the future of the earth inevitably affect and shape present attitudes to the planet. If, on the one hand, you believe that the earth is as expendable as a discarded paper cup which will be finally consumed in some cosmic combustion, then you will probably be inclined to milk the earth for all it is worth while there is time. Couple this 'theology of obliteration' with a theological attitude that the human family is not only the apex of creation but also the centre for whom all things exist, then you will act freely and without constraint to enjoy all its benefits.

If, on the other hand, you believe that the earth has a destiny in a renewed form and that the material has a place alongside the spiritual in God's eternal purposes, this will induce a more cautious attitude. Couple this with a realization that all things came into being through and for Christ, and your attitude to creation moves away from indulgence and exploitation to stewardship and reverence. Christians use the Bible to support both positions!

The Bible lays itself wide open to both interpretations. John Polkinghorne has noted in his recent book *The God of Hope and the End of the World* that throughout scripture there is a 'dialectic of eschatological continuity and discontinuity'. In other words, there are contrasting images of transience and preservation when describing the future of the earth. On the one hand 1 Thessalonians 4.16–17 and 2 Peter 3.8–13 present a dramatic future of eschatological consummation and, on the other, the prophet Isaiah paints an idealistic image of the new heavens and the new earth where 'the wolf and the lamb shall feed together' (Isaiah 65.17). Polkinghorne argues that 'some kind of balance between transience and preservation is certainly necessary' and follows Jürgen Moltmann's insistence that 'individual destinies and universal destinies are opposite sides of the same eschatological coin'. Polkinghorne concludes by stating four propositions:

1 If the universe is a creation, it must make sense everlastingly, and so ultimately it must be redeemed from transience and decay.
2 If human beings are creatures loved by their Creator, they must have a destiny beyond their deaths. (Every generation must participate equally in that destiny, in which it will receive the healing of its hurts and the restoration of its integrity, thereby participating for itself in the ultimate fulfilment of the divine purpose.)

3 In so far as present human imagination can articulate eschatological expectations, it has to do so within the tension between continuity and discontinuity. There must be sufficient continuity to ensure that individuals truly share in the life to come as their resurrected selves and not as new beings simply given the old names. There must be sufficient discontinuity to ensure that the life to come is free from the suffering and mortality of the old creation.

4 The only ground for such a hope lies in the steadfast love and faithfulness of God that is testified to by the resurrection of Jesus Christ.

In the different emphases of continuity and discontinuity Polkinghorne comes down on the side of continuity, believing that the earth has a future in a new and transformed existence. Such a view leaves it difficult to explain such cosmological passages as 2 Peter 3 where it says:

> The present heaven and earth have been reserved for fire, being kept until the day of judgement and destruction of the godless . . . the day of the Lord will come like a thief, and then the heavens will pass away with a loud noise, and the elements will be dissolved with fire, and the earth and everything that is done on it will be disclosed. (2 Peter 3.7, 10)

Interpretation of this passage hinges on the experience of fire, and basically there are two views. Fire is a symbol either of destruction or of a refinement. Interpreting scripture involves reading one text in the light of others. Putting together biblical texts about the future you cannot escape the language of renewal, restoration and liberation from the bondage to decay. Peter's reference to fire suggests to me a cataclysmic event of purification in the process of waiting 'for new heavens and a new earth, where righteousness is at home' (2 Peter 3.13).

Just as there is a continuity between these bodies we now inhabit and the spiritual bodies that Paul wrote of in 1 Corinthians 15, so there will be a continuity between the earth as we now know it and the new earth of the future.

Walter Wink's recent book *The Human Being* argues that the Son of Man 'functioned as a catalyst for personal and social transformation'. He also argues that the 'Son of Man' is an allusion to Ezekiel and that 'the Man' in that phrase is the divine figure seated on the Throne. 'And this is the revelation,' says Wink. 'God seems to be, as it were, human.'

In Matthew 19.27 Jesus says: 'Truly I tell you, at the renewal [*palingenesis*] of all things when the Son of Man is seated on the throne of his glory . . .' This futuristic picture of the Son of Man sees Jesus, as Walter Wink suggests, central to regeneration, to the 'Genesis again' [*palingenesis*], to the renewal of all things. Renewal involves judgement and becomes a gateway to everlasting life. The Son of Man, the second Adam, is as central a figure to the second Genesis as the first Adam was to the original Genesis.

Just as the first Adam was both lord ('dominion', Genesis 1.28) and servant of the earth ('serve', Genesis 2.15), so the second Adam Jesus came as both Lord ('Lord', John 13.13) and servant ('to serve', Mark 10.45). He declared his lordship uniquely in

John 13 (this is the only time in the Gospels he explicitly refers to himself as Lord) while doing the servant's work of washing his disciples' feet. Furthermore, when he predicts his coming again in a parable in Luke 12.35–7 he portrays himself again as the master who ministers. He is the servant/Lord at his second coming as well as his first. The Son of Man as the second Adam shares with the first Adam the character of the servant/Lord. This finds echoes in eternity, for the Son of Man revealed in Revelation 1 is none other than the Lamb who sits upon the throne – the lamb, the symbol of service, the throne, the symbol of lordship.

The earthing of heaven

In the book of Revelation, in the New Jerusalem where heaven comes down to earth, it is Jesus who occupies the centre stage and the place of Adam in the garden city wherein is to be found the Tree of Life (Revelation 22).

There is a continuous thread from Genesis 1 to Revelation 22 where the symbolic descriptions of the new earth are as earthy and as materialistic as the picture of the Garden of Eden. In the unfolding drama of God's creative work with the cosmos the bodily resurrection of Jesus is a watershed in the salvation history of God's material world. Matter matters to God. If only the spirit lived on we could relegate the material, the earthy world to be of secondary importance. But the material, physical resurrection of the Son of the One hewn from the earth reveals that God's eternal purposes embrace the physical as well as the spiritual. There is an unbreakable line from the bodily resurrection of Jesus back to the Genesis of the world and to the creation of the body as well as soul, the physical as well as the spiritual. Indeed, in scripture there is no dichotomy between matter and spirit, for the former is the creation of the latter.

There are two significant passages in the New Testament which speak of the role that Jesus has in bringing together earth and heaven. John 3 and 1 Corinthians 15 respectively portray Jesus as the Son of Man and the Second Adam who touches both heaven and earth.

> If I have told you about earthly things and you do not believe, how can you believe if I tell you about heavenly things? No one has ascended into heaven except the one who descended [to the earth] from heaven, the Son of Man. (John 3.12, 13)

> The first man was from the earth, a man of dust; the second man is from heaven. As was the man of dust, so are those who are of the dust; and as is the man of heaven, so are those who are of heaven. Just as we have borne the image of the man of dust, we will also bear the image of the man of heaven. (1 Corinthians 15.47–9)

It is Jesus the Son of Man who has come down to earth from heaven who holds together in himself both earthy things and heavenly things. The vision that is given to the prophet Ezekiel of God is of 'one like Adam'. The prophet Ezekiel is even addressed as 'the Son of Adam'. This human picture of God is painted in the very earthy colours of the one hewn from the earth. Ezekiel's vision has standing at the centre of the universe the figure of God drawn and depicted as an earthy human being. Here is the reality: heaven and earth are not to be two separated realms for ever, divided by sin and evil, for the ultimate reality is an undivided world where all things whether on earth or in heaven hold together in Jesus (see Colossians 1). He is central to the earthing of heaven and to the heavening of earth.

Heaven and earth belong together. In the scenario of the new heaven and the new earth there is no longer in the Revelation to St John any need of a temple in the city for 'The Lord God the Almighty and the Lamb' (21.22) have 'found their home among their people' (21.3). Heaven is earthed. The two are fused. Therein lies our destiny.

The place where we now live

The earthing of heaven is the divine scheme and context in which we are to learn our ethics about how we should treat the earth.

William Brown in his book *Ethos of the Cosmos* notes that the origin of the word 'ethics' comes from the Greek *ethos* which originally meant 'stall' or 'dwelling'. The word therefore signifies 'an environment that makes possible and sustains moral living'. He also draws attention to the fact that the first question put by God to Adam and Eve in the Garden is one about location and environment: 'Where are you?' God exposes their place in the environment before he challenges them with the moral question, 'What is this that you have done?' As Brown notes, ethos and ethics confirm the importance and 'the primacy of place in moral discourse'. We are called to make ourselves aware of where we are in order to weigh seriously both what we have done and what we are doing to the planet.

I have recently returned from India from the State of Orissa where I saw first hand the devastation dealt to fragile seaboard villages by the super-cyclones brought on by changes in the climate. These clouds of destruction make us aware of our own culpability in altering the planetary climate. They make me feel guilty about my own part in a lifestyle that is so cavalier about the resources we squander and about the effects that our actions can have on other parts of the world, especially the poor and vulnerable. In India I was asked to open a specially built cyclone shelter/Community Centre in a village whose population had been decimated by the cyclones and whose children had drowned in the floods. I cannot believe that their fate is a matter of indifference to God, nor can I believe that their conditions and those of the millions and millions of environmental refugees are peripheral to the gospel and to God's will being done on earth as in heaven.

It makes me want to repent of my own irresponsible greed. It causes me to pause in Psalm 148 where the creatures of the earth are summoned to praise God in the company of 'hail, snow and frost, stormy wind fulfilling his command' and to wonder who now is in command of the wind and the storm clouds.

It makes me long for the better clouds that will accompany the Son of Man when he reclaims the earth and fulfils his own prayer that God's will be done on earth as it is in heaven. This destiny for the earth must inform all that we do to it. We are earth's servants as well as its rulers (Genesis 1.26 and 2.15). Christ alone is Lord of all the earth.

To desecrate the earth and despoil the soil is not just a crime against humanity, it is a blasphemy, for it is to undo the creative and redemptive work of God in Christ. All things came into being not for us but for him. That is the testimony of scripture. This is the grand and divine 'plan for the fullness of time, to gather up all things in him, things in heaven and things on earth' (Ephesians 1.10).

At the end of the Oxford conference the scientists issued a statement saying that human-induced climate change is a moral, ethical and religious issue:

- God created the earth, and continues to sustain it. Made in God's image, human beings are to care for people and all creation as God cares for them. The call to 'love the Lord your God and love your neighbour' (Matthew 22.37–9) takes on new implications in the face of present and projected climate change. God has demonstrated his commitment to creation in the incarnation and resurrection of Jesus Christ. Christ who 'reconciles all things' (Colossians 1.20) calls his followers to the 'ministry of reconciliation' (2 Corinthians 5.18, 19).
- Human-induced climate change poses a great threat to the common good, especially to the poor, the vulnerable and future generations.
- By reducing the earth's biological diversity, human-induced climate change diminishes God's creation.

A parable

Imagine that somebody invites you for the cruise of a lifetime. You come to the Pier Head in Liverpool and the person says to you, 'Just a couple of conditions; this is all on me but you are never to ask where we are going or when we are going to get there.'

'Sounds fine by me,' you say. You board this ship and it's luxurious; you are shown to your suite on A-deck and you cannot believe it. Within a few hours you are sailing in the sun and you think, 'If there's a heaven, it must be like this!' After six weeks of sailing around on this ship you think to yourself, 'I wonder where we're going?' but, after all, you've made a promise and being British – stiff upper lip! – you keep the question to yourself and you carry on enjoying yourself.

After six months you cannot hold the question any longer. You grab your host one day and say, 'Listen, I don't want to appear ungrateful but please, could you just tell me where are we going and when are we going to get there?' He says, 'Is there a problem? Is the suite not comfortable? Is the food not to your liking?' 'No, no,' you say. 'It is all wonderful. I'm having the time of my life but I just wondered where and when.' He says dismissively, 'Eat, drink, be merry.' So you do your best.

After ten years of sailing around on this wretched ocean liner the dream has become a nightmare. You scream at him, 'Please, please tell me where and when.' Ridiculous? No. We are on this planet like a ship cruising through space and every now and again the question pops into the mind of every single traveller at some stage: where and when? These are questions of purpose and meaning.

Imagine you recover your composure and you say to your host, 'Well tell me, how many on this ship?' He says to you, 'Guess.' Well, you're not in the mood for guessing games and you say, 'Two hundred?' 'Wrong – a thousand.' You say, 'A thousand people? You're kidding me; it feels like two hundred'. 'Yes,' he says. 'That is what it feels like to you because here on A-deck there are only 200 people. But for the last ten years in the hold of this ship there have been 800 people and they are all on bread and water.'

Ridiculous? No. On this ship, planet Earth, 20 per cent of us are on A-deck and 80 per cent are in the hold of the ship. I have seen it in Africa and India and not so far away, and the water is not even pure.

I use that story a lot, especially in schools. It provokes several reactions. One, it is a story about privilege; two, it is a story about justice. It evokes a moral response: it begins to point up how it ought to be rather than how it is. It also induces – and this is not a fashionable concept in today's world, but here goes – guilt. There is good guilt and bad guilt. Bad guilt leads to worthlessness and low self-esteem; good guilt evokes moral responsibility and moral action.

Speaking of the future, Jesus the Son of Man said, 'In as much as you have not done it to the least of these my brothers and sisters you have not done it to me.' If you believe that the future of the earth and the plight of the least, the last and the lost is not a matter of indifference to God, then it is right to feel guilty, to repent and to act.

The alternative suggested by Jesus is an alarming scenario. You have only to read the whole of Matthew 25 to the end.

The parable continues

Imagine a great storm whips up the seas and a huge gale threatens the survival of the ship. You and your host and the passengers on A-deck take to the limited number of lifeboats and abandon ship, leaving the 800 to perish in the storm. Once you have cast adrift and at a safe distance from the impending wreckage the weather takes a surprising and immediate turn. The winds subside and as you bob around uncharted waters in your precarious little rafts you watch the abandoned ship disappear over the horizon of gold-spangled clouds into a very different future.

Discussion

Questions for further reflection on your own or with others.

1 *'One moment captivated by the beauty of the earth, the next hell-bent on filling the widening gap between need and greed.' Can you give examples of this tension in your own life?*

2 *Return to Psalm 148. How would you describe the relationship of the human family with the rest of creation?*

3 *What does the animal kingdom tell us of how God has ordered the world?*

4 *In Tennyson's poem 'In Memoriam' he writes of nature 'red in tooth and claw'. How do we square romantic notions of nature with its realities?*

5 *'In the remote past, human actions were trivial
   when set against the dominant processes of
   nature.' How has this changed?*

6 *'The beliefs that a person holds about the future
   of the earth inevitably affect and shape present
   attitudes to the earth.' How true is that of your
   own lifestyle?*

7 *'The earthing of heaven is the divine scheme and
   context in which we are to learn our ethics about
   how we should treat the earth.' How new a
   thought is this? What difference does it make
   personally and politically?*

8 *In a group provide 16 tokens numbered 31 to 46.
   Read Matthew 25.31–46 then invite people to
   pick a token blind. Whatever number they choose
   they read that verse and comment on it for no
   more than a minute.*

Chapter 4

The Son of Man Is the One Who Sows the Good Seed

The parable of the sower

I have never really understood the parable of the sower. I could not fathom why a farmer who knew his land would sow and waste precious seed in soil he knew to be so unproductive. Why sow where you know the earth was shallow or the soil full of rocks and thistles?

It was not until I went to India with Christian Aid at the end of my study leave to visit environmental projects that I saw a scene similar to the one drawn by Jesus in the parable. From a centre in Calcutta Dr Ardhentu Chatterjee and his team work in the remote villages of West Bengal, especially with those called the Landless. These are people born into poverty who have no land and have no prospect of ever owning any land. They possess nothing to sustain their lives except perhaps a few animals. By agreement with the village and the government they are allowed to grow whatever they can in that strip of no man's land that borders the road from Bengal to Bangladesh. In this narrow strip between the road and the landowners' fields they sow the seedlings of a bush that grows as rapidly as two metres in one year. They harvest this crop for two purposes: fodder for their animals and fuel with which to cook.

Shortly after I returned from India I was in one of our many Urban Priority Area Parishes in Liverpool and preaching on the parable of the sower. As I was struggling and praying to see the relevance of this rural story to the lives of the urban poor, into my mind came flashes of pictures of the landless of West Bengal eking out a living by the roadside where they sowed their seedlings. Some, of course, fell on the road, some fell in that rocky patch between the road and someone's field, some fell on the shallow earth on the edge of the road, and every now and again the seed would find some good soil and shoot up to produce a surprising crop. As I returned to the text of the parable I saw that the story Jesus told was not, after all, about a farmer but simply about a person who went out to sow. The person Jesus had in mind was less a landowning farmer and more a landless peasant for whom the sowing of the seed between the road and the field was a matter of life and death.

In Matthew's version of this story about the earth which is grouped with the parables of the weeds among the wheat, the mustard seed and the yeast, Jesus explores their meaning. In particular he explains and reveals the identity of the one who sows the good seed: it is none other than the Son of Man. Here is Jesus, the Son of Man, who, unlike the foxes who have their holes in the earth and the birds of heaven who have their nests, has nowhere to lay his head. This rootless Son of Man lives the life of the landless and dispossessed. With the rural poor and the urban poor he is one with them.

Judgement and mercy

In the same passage in Matthew 13 Jesus, the Son of Man, is again identified with justice and judgement at the end of the age and with the rooting out of all causes of sin and all evil-doers on the face of the earth. Some in the Church say that judgement is an Old Testament concept of God and that they prefer the New Testament picture of a God of Love. The truth is that there is much reference to divine judgement in the Gospels and on the lips of Jesus. To those who say, 'How can a God of love judge?', the answer must be, 'How can a God of love not judge?' If you love someone you would not stand idly by to see them abused and oppressed. Love must act against the oppressor. That is judgement. The history of social justice, social action and social reform is predicated on such a moral principle and imperative of acting against the oppressor and righting wrongs in favour of the oppressed.

As we saw in the first chapter, the idea that love must act in justice and judgement to defend the weak and vulnerable and against the oppressor lies firmly behind the popular question, 'Well, if there is a God of love why doesn't he do something about the state of the world?' What people are asking for is that God should divide the world between the good and the bad and remove all those who have contributed to the sum of human misery and turmoil.

It is a fair and compassionate question to put to God. But the truth is that such a question leaves us all gasping for the oxygen of divine forgiveness. Whenever we press for the God of justice to judge between the good and the bad and act against the latter we are

71

left pleading for a God of mercy to forgive us our sins and trespasses.

It is in the person of Jesus that we meet with God as both Judge and Saviour. 'The Father judges no one but has given all judgement to the Son . . . he has given him authority to execute judgement because he is the Son of Man' (John 5.22, 27). The Son of Man who exercises judgement is also the Son of Man who has 'authority on earth to forgive' (Matthew 2.10). We are judged by the goodness of his life and are utterly dependent on his gift of forgiveness which, through the cross, he readily bestows on all who come to him.

Scenes of judgement and mercy crowd the pages of the book of Revelation as the curtain is pulled back on the window into heaven:

The seventh angel sounded his trumpet, and there were loud voices in heaven, which said:

'The kingdom of the world has become the kingdom of our Lord and of his Christ, and he will reign for ever and ever.'

And the twenty-four elders, who were seated on their thrones before God, fell on their faces and worshipped God, saying:

'We give thanks to you, Lord God Almighty,
who is and who was,
because you have taken your great power and
have begun to reign.
The nations were angry;
and your wrath has come.
The time has come for judging the dead,

and for rewarding your servants the prophets
and your saints and those who reverence your
name,
both small and great –
and for destroying those who destroy the earth'.

Then God's temple in heaven was opened, and
within his temple was seen the ark of his covenant.
And there came flashes of lightning, rumblings,
peals of thunder, an earthquake and a great hail-
storm. (Revelation 11.15–19, NIV; italics mine)

The earth quakes here at the time of judgement as it
did at both the crucifixion and resurrection of Jesus.
In this vision it is spelt out explicitly how God will
act decisively against 'those who destroy the earth'
(Revelation 11.18).

This further demonstrates God's commitment to
the earth and all that he has made. It takes you back
from the last book in the Bible to the first and to
Genesis 9 when God makes his Covenant in a pledge
to Noah:

And God said, 'This is the sign of the covenant I
am making between me and you and every living
creature with you, a covenant for all generations
to come: I have set my rainbow in the clouds, and
it will be the sign of the covenant between me *and
the earth'.* (Genesis 9.12–13, NIV; italics mine)

The covenant is not just between God and Noah but
with 'every living creature of all flesh that is on the
earth' and with the very earth itself. Like the Ark of
the Covenant, the earth is the holy footstool of God.

It is sacred. The earth is not personified or deified in the Bible. But by the virtue of the creation, the covenant and the cross it is consecrated and sanctified by God the Creator and reconciled to God the Redeemer of the universe.

Personal and cosmic

> For he has rescued us from the dominion of darkness and brought us into the kingdom of the Son he loves, in whom we have redemption, the forgiveness of sins. He is the image of the invisible God, the firstborn over all creation. For by him all things were created: things in heaven and on earth, visible and invisible, whether thrones or powers or rulers or authorities; all things were created by him and for him. He is before all things, and in him all things hold together. And he is the head of the body, the church; he is the beginning and the firstborn, from among the dead, so that in everything he might have the supremacy. For God was pleased to have all his fullness dwell in him and through him to reconcile to himself all things, whether things on earth or things in heaven, by making peace through his blood, shed on the cross. (Colossians 1.13–20, NIV)

In this remarkable passage in Paul's letter there are two emphases that call for attention regarding the subject of this book: the personal and the cosmic. 'For he has rescued us from the dominion of darkness and brought us into the kingdom of the Son he loves, in whom we have redemption, the forgiveness of sins' (13, 14). Forgiveness is an intensely personal experience. It both expresses and encourages intimacy in a relationship. Think of any moment when you have been reconciled with another through genuine sorrow and forgiveness and you will know the power of such grace to restore a broken relationship. If that is true of human relationships it is all the more true in our relationship with God. I know that some of the deepest moments of communion with God come to me when I find myself again at the foot of the cross, confessing my sin and finding him faithful and just, forgiving me and cleansing me from all unrighteousness. I love that old hymn:

> Just as I am, without one plea
> but that thy blood was shed for me,
> and that thou bidst me come to thee,
> O Lamb of God, I come.

And with David from Psalm 51 I often pray:

Have mercy on me, O God,
according to your unfailing love;
according to your great compassion
blot out my transgressions.
Wash away all my iniquity
and cleanse me from my sin.
For I know my transgressions,
for my sin is always before me.
Against you, you only, have I sinned
and done what is evil in your sight,
so that you are proved right when you speak
and justified when you judge. (verses 1–4, NIV)

The appeal to God's steadfast love and abundant mercy is the beginning of the restoration of that relationship of intimacy with God. Allegri's *Miserere*, his exquisite setting to music of Psalm 51, evokes both the depths and heights of such divine love.

David's sins are well known. Betrayal, abuse of power, connivance to murder, adultery – these are some of the transgressions and sins 'ever before me'. In the Sermon on the Mount Jesus radicalizes the moral law of the Old Testament by applying the Ten Commandments not just to our actions but also to the thoughts of our hearts. Beneath the searching eye of God and compared with the perfect life of Jesus 'we have all sinned and fallen short of the glory of God'.

When it comes to sin we naturally think first of those thoughts and deeds that wreak havoc in our immediate circle. But the Bible gives personal sin a much wider radius, encompassing our complicity on a broader canvas.

Through the prophet Isaiah God calls to us with grace:

'Come now, let us reason together,' says the LORD.
'Though your sins are like scarlet,
they shall be as white as snow;
though they are red as crimson,
they shall be like wool.' (Isaiah 1.18, NIV)

Elsewhere in the chapter he lists some of the scarlet sins and paints a picture of a society that has exchanged justice for cheating and bribery and abandoned the orphan and the widow.

'Wash yourselves; make yourselves clean;
remove the evil of your doings from before my
eyes;
cease to do evil,
learn to do good;
seek justice,
rescue the oppressed,
defend the orphan,
plead for the widow.

How the faithful city has become a whore!
She that was full of justice,
righteousness lodged in her – but now murderers!
Your silver has become dross,
your wine is mixed with water.
Your princes are rebels
and companions of thieves.
Everyone loves a bribe
and runs after gifts.
They do not defend the orphan,
and the widow's cause does not come before them.'
(Isaiah 1.16–17 and 21–3)

The truth is that given the complexity of human society we are all complicit in the social sins of injustice and world poverty. 'Ah,' we might say, prepared to take the rap for our individual transgressions but unconvinced of our complicity in the plight of the disadvantaged globally. 'When did we ever cause the poor to go hungry or displace the asylum seeker?' Before pressing the question too far we do well to recall again how Jesus answered a similar question: 'Truly I tell you, just as you did not do it to one of the least of these, you did not do it to me.'

This disturbing and familiar passage in Matthew 25.31–46 finds Jesus in reflective and prophetic mood predicting what will happen when he 'the Son of Man comes in glory'. As he casts himself as the Son of Man again in the role of judge of the nations, the sins of society are clearly both individual and communal. The sins for which we need God's forgiveness are both personal and social.

This brings me to the second emphasis in Paul's letter to the Colossians. Redemption and reconciliation encompass not just individual souls but 'all things, whether on earth or in heaven'. Although, as I have already testified, there is a deep spiritual experience to be had by individual sinners at the foot of the cross of Jesus Christ and one which is essential to salvation, the scope of the benefit of 'the blood of his cross' encompasses 'all things whether on earth or in heaven'. Creation is cosmic and so is salvation. By this I mean that since 'all things in heaven and on earth . . . have been created through him and for him' then it follows that he who 'sustains all things by his powerful word' (Hebrews 1.3) should not abandon his creation but out of love 'reconcile to himself all things, whether on earth or in heaven'. This is, indeed, good news. The earth is safe, not because of human ingenuity but saved because of God's faithfulness expressed in a trinity of divine actions – the creation, the covenant and the cross – in relation to the earth.

Regeneration and restoration

The earth has a future within the redemptive purpose of God and this is expressed throughout the Old and the New Testaments in the phrase 'the new earth', which will be accompanied by 'new heavens'. Tom Wright's book on the resurrection (*The Resurrection of the Son of God*) and Tony Thiselton's commentary on 1 Corinthians 15 (*The First Epistle to the Corinthians*) offer an exploration of how the New Testament envisages the future. Disembodied spirits and a dematerialized earth are not part of the biblical vision! In 1 Corinthians 15 Paul writes of a 'spiritual body' which is the gift of Jesus 'the last Adam'. The difference between the physical bodies of which we are now constituted and our spiritual bodies following the resurrection of the dead is that the former are perishable and the latter imperishable (1 Corinthians 5.42). The difference is not one of materiality or bodiness!

The 'new earth' too is not a dematerialized existence. There will be a 'regeneration [*palingenesis*] of all things' when the Son of Man comes in glory, and those who have forsaken material things such as houses or families or fields for the sake of following Jesus will receive them all back *in greater measure* as they inherit eternal life. This vision of the future painted by Jesus, the Son of Man, is thoroughly earthy and, what is more, materialistic!

> Then Peter said in reply, 'Look, we have left everything and followed you. What then will we have?' Jesus said to them, 'Truly I tell you, at the renewal of all things, when the Son of Man is seated on the throne of his glory, you who have followed me will also sit on twelve thrones, judging the twelve tribes of Israel. And everyone who has left houses or brothers or sisters or father or mother or children or fields for my name's sake, will receive a hundredfold, and will inherit eternal life.' (Matthew 19.27–9)

This is echoed in Peter's sermon in Acts 3 when he preaches:

> Repent therefore, and turn to God, so that your sins may be wiped out, so that times of refreshing may come from the presence of the Lord, and that he may send the Messiah appointed for you, that is Jesus, who must remain in heaven until the time of universal restoration that God announced long ago through his holy prophets.

This 'time of universal restoration' is surely what he and his followers had in mind when praying for the coming of the good Father's Kingdom and the doing of God's will on earth as it is done in heaven. The earthing of heaven is a materialistic vision where to pray for it leads naturally in the next breath to ask for daily bread.

Paul explains in Romans 5 that the first Adam through his sin and disobedience infected the human race and blighted and mortally wounded the whole world; Jesus, the second Adam, the Son of Man, the Son of God, both hewn from the earth and come down from heaven, becomes the means of grace, abounding grace, so that his free gift of forgiveness restores the human race to righteousness, to justice and to eternal life. The question that continues to intrigue me is that if Paul was clear that in the divine scheme of things Jesus was the second Adam, was Jesus himself aware of this relationship with Adam?

In the first chapter I looked at three contexts where Jesus speaks of himself as the Son of Man in relation to the earth. When it comes to the meaning of the Son of Man I am persuaded by Walter Wink (see *The Human Being*) that when using the title Jesus draws on many strands and heavily on the imagery of Ezekiel. In the opening 'vision of God' to the Son of Man (Ben Adam) there appears one seated above the dome on a throne who significantly has the form of Adam, a human being (Ezekiel 1.26). Ezekiel, the Son of Man, is convinced that this vision of Adam is none other than the Lord himself!

> Above the expanse over their heads was what looked like a throne of sapphire, and high above on the throne was a figure *like that of a man.* I saw that from what appeared to be his waist up he looked like glowing metal, as if full of fire, and that from there down he looked like fire; and brilliant light surrounded him. Like the appearance of a rainbow in the clouds on a rainy day, so was the radiance around him. (Ezekiel 1.26–8, NIV; italics mine)

The vision in Ezekiel is therefore of God in human form, the perfect Adam. When Ezekiel constantly hears himself addressed as Son of Man (Ben Adam) he could be forgiven for thinking that the title 'Son of Man/Ben Adam' spoke of his spiritual relationship with the Lord who had the appearance of Adam.

I wonder too whether when Jesus spoke of himself as 'Son of Man' or simply as the Son he did not also see this as speaking both of his relationship to Adam formed in the image of God and to God himself in whose image Adam and all his successors are made. As we have seen from Luke's genealogy the Son of Man has a lineage that goes all the way back to 'the Son of Adam, the Son of God' (Luke 3.38). Jesus as Son of Man and Son of God is the one who holds together both earth and heaven in his very person.

The garden

The renewal and restoration of all things that the Son of Man talks about in Matthew 19 is dramatically envisaged in Ezekiel 36:

> Thus says the LORD God: 'On the day that I cleanse you from all your iniquities . . . the land that was desolate shall be tilled . . . and they will say 'This land that was desolate has become like the garden of Eden'.

Adam's Eden is the vision of what God will again accomplish. Ezekiel sees Adam's garden as the antithesis of the 'waste places' and the 'desolation' that characterize the earth dominated by people of 'evil ways', whose dealings 'were not good' and who were loathsome for their 'iniquities' and 'abominable deeds' (Ezekiel 36.31–5). Adam's Eden is the Son of Man's ideal world. His garden, the one planted by God (Genesis 2.8), is the model of the new world that is coming when God will deal decisively with all that spoils the soil, desecrates his creation, undermines his covenant and causes the cross.

The image of the restored garden is repeated in the prophecies of Isaiah:

> For the LORD will comfort Zion; he will comfort all her waste places, and will make her wilderness like Eden, her desert like the garden of the LORD; joy and gladness will be found in her, thanksgiving and the voice of song. (Isaiah 51.3)

> The LORD will guide you continually, and satisfy
> your needs in parched places, and make your
> bones strong; and you shall be like a watered
> garden, like a spring of water, whose waters never
> fail. (Isaiah 58.11)

It is often said that the Bible begins with a garden and ends with a city. Although that is an affirmation of urban life it does not tell the whole story. The truth is that the book of Revelation gives us a picture of a garden city at the end. The vision of the New Jerusalem is of a city where 'the river of the water of life, bright as crystal, flows through the middle of the street' and 'on either side of the river is the tree of life, with its twelve kinds of fruit . . . and the leaves of the tree are for the healing of the nations'. This heavenly city has shades of Eden and puts me in mind of Dr Johnson's saying that heaven would contain the joys of the countryside and the amenities of the town!

Gethsemane

Significant episodes in the life of Jesus occur in a garden – Gethsemane and Golgotha. In Gethsemane, distressed and agitated at the prospect of his death, Jesus separates himself from the disciples and throws himself on the earth. As he lies there prostrate on the ground and with the length of his body feels the earth, he prays to the Father about his destiny (Mark 14.32–5).

Luke tells us in verses that do not appear in every version of the Gospel that as he prays so an angel of *heaven* comes to give him strength. Yet this does not assuage his anguish 'and his sweat became like great drops of blood falling down *on the earth*!' (Luke 22.43, 44; italics mine).

On the Mount of Olives in the Garden of Gethsemane earth and heaven are joined as the Son of Man hugs the earth in earnest prayer to the Father as an angel ministers to him from heaven.

Matthew, Mark and Luke all tell the story differently. Mark alone tells us that Jesus stretched himself out on the earth. Luke alone tells us Jesus was given strength by an angel from heaven. Prostrate in prayer Jesus, like a lightning conductor, becomes the conduit of the grace of heaven to the earth itself. It is almost a parable of his entire mission and ministry. After he has been strengthened by the angel of heaven the beads of sweat, like drops of blood, fall to water the earth itself. It is a sign that his lonely labours which caused him such distress and agitation would be for the renewing of the earth.

Golgotha

As on the Mount of Transfiguration the Garden of Gethsemane becomes a place of mediation between earth and heaven. The Garden of Golgotha where Jesus is buried also becomes on the day of resurrection a meeting place of heaven and earth. John the Evangelist tells us that when Mary reaches the grave she encounters two angels in the tomb. Having asked her why she is weeping she complains that she does not know where people have taken her Lord. She turns around and although she does not recognize him sees Jesus standing there. John continues, 'Jesus said to her, "Woman, why are you weeping? Whom are you looking for?" Supposing him to be the gardener, she said . . .'

At the same time as giving the Galt Lectures in America I was also asked to lead a seminar on 'Faith and Sustainable Development' at the World Bank in association with Peter Harris of A Rocha, an international environmental charity. After I had set forward the ideas in the first chapter about the possibility of the earthy roots of the phrase 'Son of Man', one of the participants asked if I thought this accounted for why Mary mistook Jesus for the gardener. Who knows? But it is one of those imponderables that is fun to ponder! What was it about the Risen Christ that made her think he was a gardener? After all, there were two angels present with whom she did not make the same mistake. Was there an earthiness about even his risen demeanour that made her think that this was a man of the soil? The stone of the tomb had been rolled away not to let Jesus out (he could move through walls in his resurrected body); the tomb was opened to let Mary and the other disciples in to see what had happened to Jesus after his death. Whatever she saw made her think that this person standing before her was none other than the gardener of Golgotha.

As I have reflected on the question at the World Bank seminar and meditated on the biblical images of gardens I have come to the conclusion that Mary, in fact, made no mistake at all! When she set eyes on the Risen Jesus she did see the gardener. Perhaps it is yet another example of the famous ironies in John's Gospel. Just as Pontius Pilate, when asking Jesus 'What is truth?' did not realize that the answer was literally staring him in the face, so Mary, supposing the man before her was a gardener, did not realize that Jesus, the second Adam, was indeed the gardener of the new Eden.

Through the rebellion of Adam and Eve the whole human race is infected with sin and the whole earth affected by human exploitation. The earth is cursed and gradually becomes a wilderness blighted by human greed. Only through the repentance and absolution of the human race, 'ransomed, healed, restored, forgiven', can the wastelands and the wildernesses become again as the Son of Man prophesized in Ezekiel like the Garden of Eden.

The first gardener was not Adam but God. 'And the Lord God planted a garden in Eden, in the east; and there he put the man whom he had formed. Out of the ground the Lord God made to grow every tree that is pleasant to the sight and good for food . . .' (Genesis 2.8, 9).

God, the first gardener, sent his son, 'the last Adam' and the last gardener to inaugurate the new heavens and the new earth and 'to reconcile to himself all things, whether on earth or in heaven, by making peace through the blood of his cross' (Colossians 1.20). It was the gardener, after all, that Mary saw, the one who in the Revelation to John, sits at the centre of the garden city of the new Jerusalem saying, 'See, I am making all things new.' Adam, the first gardener after God, cursed the earth; Jesus, the last Adam and the last gardener, blesses the earth – with his sweat falling into it, with his body prostrate on it, with his blood shed for it and for us all on the cross.

Justice

In one of the new Eucharistic Prayers of *Common Worship* the Minister pleads with God for the future of the earth:

Bless the earth
Heal the sick
Let the oppressed go free.

This vision of the coming of the good Father's Kingdom and the doing of God's will on earth is consonant with all the dimensions of the vision given by God to the Son of Man in Ezekiel. The earthing of heaven has God the true and good shepherd making his sheep lie down with the pledge: 'I will seek the lost, and I will bring back the strayed, and I will bind up the injured, and I will strengthen the weak, but the fat and the strong I will destroy. I will feed them with justice' (Ezekiel 34.16).

The food of God's justice is nutritious and complex. In Romans 5 where Paul compares the fatal consequences of Adam's sin with the vital benefits of Jesus' obedience (Romans 5.1–21) he expounds righteousness and justification. Through the death of Jesus 'we are justified by faith, we have peace with God', 'rarely will one die for a righteous person, but God proves his love for us that while we still were sinners Christ died for us', 'now that we have been justified by his blood', 'For the judgement following one trespass brought condemnation, but the free gift following many trespasses brings justification', 'one man's act of righteousness leads to justification and life for all', 'by one man's obedience the many will be made righteous', 'justification leading to eternal life through Jesus Christ our Lord'.

However one interprets the letter to the Romans these verses lead to the inescapable conclusion that God through Jesus Christ's death makes us sinners who wreck the earth at one with him in his righteousness and justice. God feeds us with justice as he promised in Ezekiel by making us one with him. Such at-one-ness with the justice of God can never be solely a matter of personal salvation. It is, of course, personal in that we experience this justification, this peace with God, this love, this reconciliation, this grace, this righteousness, this eternal life in the depth of our own being. But if it is God's justice that we enter into, that we experience through our personal relationship with Jesus Christ, we are necessarily caught up in God's holy desire for justice on the earth. You cannot be in a right relationship with the God of justice and be indifferent to the injustice that is in the world. That is a contradiction of terms. You cannot say that you love the God of justice and at the same time turn a blind eye to the injustices that are an offence to his character.

To be fed by God's justice is to be sustained by the God who says, 'I will seek the lost, and I will bring back the strayed, and I will bind up the injured, and I will strengthen the weak, but the fat and the strong I will destroy.'

The justice of God is committed to righting wrongs and bringing the human family back into a right relationship with himself and into a right and harmonious relationship with each other.

I have to confess that being nurtured in the evangelical tradition I and others have not always readily grasped the biblical connection between the doctrine of justification by faith and the making of a just society. Yet the two belong together. To plagiarize a verse from the letter of John, who was not averse to calling people liars, and who wrote: 'Those who say, "I love God" and hate their brothers or sisters are liars'

(1 John 4.20), we could add, 'Those who say that we can be justified by faith and love the God of justice while ignoring the injustices inflicted upon the last, the least and the lost make God out to be a liar.' The strictures of Jesus, God's own righteousness revealed in human flesh, show that to disregard the injustices of the poor is to disregard him (Matthew 25).

Although old barriers are breaking down there are still divisions among Christians over emphases in the Gospels. Those who seek to win people to a personal faith in Jesus Christ through emphasizing the priority of being justified by faith are often slow to show the equal priority of working with the God of justice in the world. And those who see as their priority the call to challenge unjust structures and create a just society can sometimes be slow to see the equal priority of being brought into a right relationship with the God of justice through the atoning death of Jesus Christ.

One of the conundrums of modern Christianity is that evangelicals who have emphasized the importance of the bodily resurrection of Jesus have been weak in their proclamation of the material aspects of the Gospels. Liberals, on the other hand, who have held fast to the social and material dimensions of the Kingdom have been reluctant to declare the material aspect of the bodily resurrection of Jesus. The Bible presents us with a mission of God that is holistic, i.e. spiritual and physical, personal and social, individual and corporate. When in the synagogue in Nazareth Jesus read and preached from the prophet Isaiah he was in no doubt that the spiritual experience of being anointed by the Spirit had physical consequences in preaching good news to the poor (Luke 4.18, 19). He forgave people their sins, he healed the blind like

Bartimaeus, he so transformed the life of Zacchaeus that the rich tax collector gave half his possessions to the poor and made quadruple restitution to the people he had defrauded and in so doing began to let the oppressed go free. A right relationship with the God of righteousness went hand in hand with feeding people, especially the poor, with justice.

Indeed, at the end of the Nazareth manifesto Jesus, quoting Isaiah, says that he has come 'to proclaim the year of the Lord's favour'. What was this? The year of Jubilee. Although Jubilee has rightly been associated as a time to cancel debts it was originally given as a land ordinance, a time for the earth to rest.

> And you shall hallow the fiftieth year and you shall proclaim liberty throughout the land to all its inhabitants. It shall be a jubilee for you: you shall return, every one of you, to your property and everyone of you to your family. That fiftieth year shall be a jubilee for you: you shall not sow, or reap the aftergrowth, or harvest the unpruned vines. For it is a jubilee; it shall be holy to you; you shall eat only what the field itself produces. (Leviticus 25.10–12)

The Sabbath too, like the Jubilee, was to ensure 'complete rest for the land' (Leviticus 25.4) otherwise the earth would become exhausted and infertile and the people spiral downwards into poverty.

Sabbath and Jubilee are given by God to order and ensure a world of sustainable sufficiency. There are some Christians who spiritualize and dematerialize the Nazareth manifesto, arguing that its application is simply a spiritual metaphor, denying that it has any social or political application either to the ministry of Jesus or to the mission of God today. But Jesus had a material ministry – he fed the hungry, he cured the blind, he raised the dead, he healed the sick, he inspired crowds, he influenced individuals on how they used power, spent money and had sex. His attitude to creation was consonant with the opening chapter of Genesis that everything God had made was 'good'. He of all people knew the power of evil and the reality of sin and the devastating effects these had on the material world. But his knowledge was a spur to him urging us to pray not that we should escape the earth but that the earth should be again the place where God's will is done as perfectly as it is done in heaven.

Yet for many Christians Christianity has taken the form of escapology. Evangelism has been skewed and reduced to providing converts with an escape route from the earth and a prospect to bagging a place in heaven. We have lost sight of that vision of the Kingdom which arrested the hearts and minds of the New Testament Christians when Peter preached to them:

> Repent therefore, and turn to God, so that your sins may be wiped out, so that times of refreshing may come from the presence of the Lord, and that he may send the Messiah appointed for you, that is Jesus, who must remain in heaven until the time of universal restoration that God announced long ago through his holy prophets. (Acts 3.19–21)

'The time of universal restoration' is the same as 'the renewal of all things, when the Son of Man is seated on the throne of glory'. This is for what the ascended

Jesus must yet remain in heaven. This is for what we wait and towards which we work as we pray for the earthing of heaven, the doing of God's will on earth as in heaven.

A corner of creation

As a Bishop in the Church of England I believe that God has given us an important heritage through the network of parishes. A parish is a corner of God's creation, a small enclosure within the garden of the earth. Within this boundary we have a responsibility for 'the cure of souls', not just of the gathered congregation but of all who live within the parish boundary. Together with other Christians and with people of good will we work within this boundary for the holistic transformation of the neighbourhood, for its regeneration spiritually and physically. As we encourage others to learn Christ with us we open ourselves to that transforming power of his Spirit that enables us to pray and to work for the earthing of heaven. The parish is the arena for the earthing of heaven locally. That is our local mission. World mission is the earthing of heaven globally.

I worry about the undermining of the parish in today's Church. We seem to be discarding a God-given opportunity just at the time that other people are becoming increasingly sceptical about centralization and globalization and increasingly persuaded by the merits of localization. Although I am a supporter of the emerging Church, of being Church in a new way and of church planting, I want to resist the encroachments of the commuter church where crowds of Christians drive miles in their cars often past deprived areas to worship in a smart building sometimes located in a poor part of town. Christians come and go but seldom connect with the people who live in the community around the building. How are they to experience the Good News? What opportunities are being lost of earthing the gospel in that neighbourhood?

It seems a long way from the Son of Man who sowed his seeds in the earth and on the edge.

> Glory be to God for dappled things –
> For skies of couple-colour as a brinded cow;
> For rose-moles all in stipple upon trout that swim;
> Fresh-firecoal chestnut-falls; finches' wings;
> Landscape plotted and pieced – fold, fallow, and
> plough;
> And all trades, their gear and tackle and trim.
> All things counter, original, spare, strange;
> Whatever is fickle, freckled (who knows how?)
> With swift, slow; sweet, sour; adazzle, dim;
> He fathers-forth whose beauty is past change:
> Praise him.
>
> (Gerard Manley Hopkins)

Discussion

Questions for further reflection on your own or with others.

1 *'By virtue of creation, the covenant and the cross the earth is sacred.' How do these three actions of God affect your attitude to the earth?*

2 *What are the reasons for and against finding the thought of divine judgement so unacceptable?*

3   *Look again at the passage from Colossians; where do you see the personal and the cosmic emphases?*

4   *Why do we fail to make the connection between justification by faith and the making of a just society?*

5   *In the Lord's Prayer in the Book of Common Prayer the petition reads: 'Thy will be done in earth as it is in heaven.' 'In earth' suggests the dynamic purposes of God at work not just on the face of the earth but in and through the deep and complex interconnectedness of all creation. Reflect prayerfully on 'Thy will be done in earth.'*

6. *In the Diocese of Liverpool we are appointing voluntary environmental representatives in each parish. Printed here are: (a) the guidelines on how a parish might become more environmentally responsible, and (b) the job description of the parish environmental representative.*

Guidelines on how a parish might become more environmentally responsible.

Waste
- Recycle everything (e.g. aluminium, steel, glass, and textiles, electrical goods and furniture).
- Use paper made from recycled fibre (including photocopier paper).
- Use both sides of *all* paper (including when photocopying).
- Collect reusable paper (scrap paper can be used for note-taking).

- Ensure that *all* paper is eventually saved for recycling.
- Place memos on a notice board when possible.
- Try to utilize e-mail or the phone for internal and external communication.
- Use envelopes made of recycled fibre or manila envelopes rather than heavily bleached white ones.
- Open envelopes carefully for reuse (reusable labels are available).
- Are the reusable cups and plates in daily use made of 'environment-friendly' materials?
- When disposable items can't be avoided are they recyclable or biodegradable?
- Use toilet paper made from recycled fibre.
- Buy goods in bulk to avoid excess packaging.
- Buy second-hand goods and pass on unwanted items to others.

Energy and pollution
- Are any sources of renewable energy utilized (e.g. Unite)?
- Is energy efficiency considered when purchasing appliances, favouring the A rating?
- Can reconditioned electrical 'white' goods be utilized instead of new purchases?
- Can electrical goods be upgraded rather than replaced?
- Switch off all electrical appliances when not in use (including lights, photocopiers and computers).
- Are all lights energy efficient and turned off as soon as there is sufficient daylight?
- Ensure that kettles are not overfilled.
- Is it possible to use gas for heating and cooking?

(It is more energy efficient than electricity.)
- How modern is the heating system? Instant heaters are generally more energy efficient.
- Are thermostatic controls fitted to radiators and boilers?
- Could heating be turned down by even one degree?
- Do not heat unused rooms!
- Are hot water pipes and tanks properly insulated?
- Tap water should be comfortably hot (overheated water is wasteful).
- Are hot-water taps free of drips?
- Is there loft, roof and cavity wall insulation?
- Are windows double-glazed? With low-emissivity (K) glass?
- Are windows cleaned regularly to increase level of natural light?
- Are windows and doors free from draughts?
- Are good fitting curtains with thermal linings fitted at windows?
- Are windows and doors kept closed during cold weather?
- Do all outside doors close automatically?
- Are rooms carpeted to insulate solid floors/reduce draughts?
- Are shelves fitted above radiators to deflect warm air into a room?
- Are reflector panels fitted behind radiators?

Transport
- Reduce car journeys – walk, cycle or use public transport where possible.
- When planning meetings and events consider whether shared transport and the use of public transport is a viable option.

- Could cycling be encouraged by providing dry, secure cycle storage?
- Consider emissions when purchasing vehicles.
- Is financial support for bus and cycle journeys provided in addition to mileage allowance?

Water
- Is the water pressure adjusted to be enough without being excessive?
- Are timed operation taps installed?
- Are dripping taps repaired quickly?
- Have automatic urinal flush controls been fitted?
- Can double-flush or low-flush volume WCs be installed?
- Have water hippos been installed in toilets?
- Has paying water bills by meter rather than the uniform charge been considered?
- Collect and use 'grey' water where possible.
- Are cleaning products environment friendly and biodegradable (e.g. Ecover)? In general, avoid chlorine-based bleaches, phosphate-based detergents and any cleaners not 100 per cent biodegradable.
- Try to use LESS cleaner and detergent – they all have some impact.

Grounds
- Are they free from herbicides/pesticides?
- Is there a log pile, hedgerow, shrubs, trees, nettles, birdboxes, bird feeding station?
- Is compost peat-free?
- Is organic waste from the grounds composted?
- Is domestic vegetable waste composted?
- Has hiring or borrowing of gardening and DIY tools been considered if used only occasionally?

Purchasing
- Are Fair Trade goods used?
- Are the stages of production of goods considered along with the impact this may have on environments and populations?
- Are long-life products chosen over short-life ones?
- Is the energy used for manufacture and delivery considered, e.g. is the milk delivered regularly by a milk roundsman?
- Are products locally produced?
- Are products made from tropical hardwoods avoided?
- Is all wood from sustainable sources?
- Are food labels examined to find what additives are used? Is the product GM-free?
- Are vegetarian alternatives offered?
- Consider changing to a bank with a recognized ethical policy, e.g. Co-operative Bank.

(Based on a document compiled by Wendy Boulton)

Job description of the parish environmental representative

Purpose
To mobilize the hearts, minds and resources of people in the parish to bring about recovery of and care for their local environment in ways which develop and care for people and communities to help bring about environmental, social and economic transformation and sustainability.

Main responsibilities include:

- Raise environmental awareness and promote environmental action within the parish.
- Facilitate a multi-faith approach to tackling these common environmental issues by encouraging the Deanery's parishes to work ecumenically and with other faith communities.
- Initiate and participate in the organization of events aimed at raising environmental awareness and promoting environmental action in the parish.
- Develop links with environmental organizations and other interested parties and communicate information to the Diocesan Environmental Co-ordinator to help maintain an environmental database for the Diocese.

Other responsibilities include:

- Keep abreast of current environmental issues and research.
- Contribute to the development of a Diocesan environmental website.
- Promote the adoption of sound stewardship practices on all Church of England property within the parish through the development and implementation of environmental audits and charters.
- Raise environmental awareness in clergy and laity within the parish through information and education.
- Raise environmental awareness in Church of England employees within the parish through information and education.
- Aid in the development of liturgy and preaching materials aimed at highlighting environmental issues.

- Promote environmental awareness within any Church of England controlled and aided schools within the parish and aid in the development of environmentally based activities and study materials which can be incorporated into school programmes.
- Promote environmental awareness within Church of England affiliated clubs, boards, organizations and initiatives and aid in the development of environmentally based activities and study materials.
- Embrace opportunities for training and personal development where they arise.

Though Parish Representatives will be required to work autonomously, information and co-ordination will also be provided through the Diocesan Environmental Co-ordinator. Support will be offered by the Diocesan Environmental Co-ordinator in line with the Diocesan Voluntary Policy.

The parish representative must be:

- Enthusiastic and self-motivated with the determination to initiate environmental projects and bring them to a successful conclusion.
- Committed to elevating the environmental agenda within the parish in a way which is sympathetic to the beliefs held by people of all faiths and particularly by those represented within the Church of England.
- Willing and able to spend time each week fulfilling the specified role.

To what extent could you take this forward in your own church and neighbourhood?

A Prayer
(adapted from a prayer by Henry VI)

O Lord Jesus Christ,
through and for whom all things have come into
    being,
you have created and redeemed me,
and in the company of all in heaven and on earth
have brought me unto that which now I am.
You know what you would do with me and all
    creation;
do with us according to your will
for your tender mercy's sake. Amen.

Further Reading

Beckerman, Wilfred and Pasek, Joanna *Justice, Posterity and the Environment* (Oxford University Press, 2001)

Berry, R J. *God's Book of Works* (T & T Clark, 2003)

Brown, William *Ethos of the Cosmos: The Genesis of Moral Imagination in the Bible* (Eerdmans, 1999)

Echlin, Edward *Earth Spirituality: Jesus at the Centre* (Arthur James/John Hunt Publishing, 1999)

Hawken, Paul, Lovins, Amory B., and Lovins, L. Hunter *Natural Capitalism: Creating the Next Industrial Revolution* (Little, Brown & Co., 1999)

Holdgate, Martin *From Care to Action* (Earthscan, 1996)

Houghton, John *Global Warming: The Complete Briefing* (Cambridge University Press, 1997)

Lomborg, Bjørn *The Skeptical Environmentalist: Measuring the Real State of the World* (Cambridge University Press, 2001)

McIntosh, Alastair: Submission for the Public Inquiry into the proposed super quarry on the Isle of Harris. Presented at Leverburgh, Isle of Harris, 9 November 1994

McIntosh, Alastair *Soil and Soul* (Aurum Press, 2001)

McNeill, John *Something New Under the Sun* (W. W. Norton, 2000)

Polkinghorne, John *The God of Hope and the End of the World* (SPCK, 2002)

Porritt, Jonathon *Playing Safe: Science and the Environment* (Thames & Hudson, 2000)

Rees, Martin *Our Final Century: Will the Human Race Survive the 21st Century?* (Heinemann, 2003)

Sarkar, R. L. *The Bible, Ecology and Environment* (ISPCK, 2000)

Temple, William *Nature, Man and God* (Gifford Lectures) (Macmillan, 1934)

Thiselton, Anthony *The First Epistle to the Corinthians* (Eerdmans Paternoster, 2001)

White, Lyn 'The Historical Roots of Our Ecologic Crisis', *Science*, 115 (1967)

Wink, Walter *The Human Being: Jesus and the Enigma of the Son of Man* (Fortress Press, 2001)

Wright, N. T. *The Resurrection of the Son of God* (SPCK, 2003)